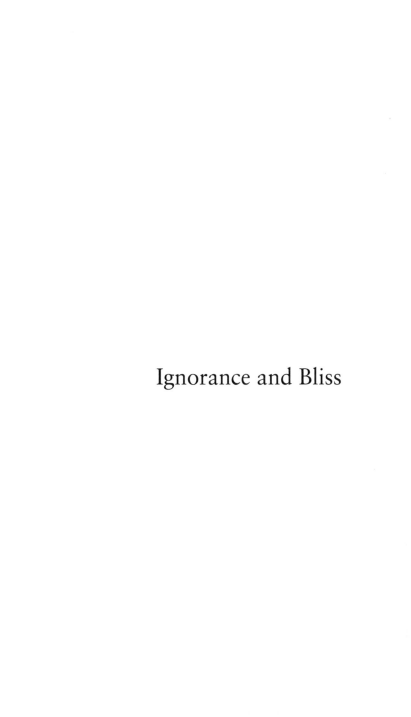

Ignorance and Bliss

Ignorance and Bliss

ON WANTING NOT TO KNOW

Mark Lilla

HURST & COMPANY, LONDON

Published in the United States in 2024 by Farrar, Straus and Giroux

First published in the United Kingdom in 2024 by
C. Hurst & Co. (Publishers) Ltd.,
New Wing, Somerset House, Strand, London, WC2R 1LA

A Cataloguing-in-Publication data record for this book
is available from the British Library.

ISBN: 9781911723523

This book is printed using paper from registered sustainable
and managed sources.

Printed and bound in Great Britain by Bell & Bain Ltd, Glasgow

www.hurstpublishers.com

An early version of chapter 4 was published as "Lambs and
Wolves" in *Liberties* (Autumn 2021). An early version of
chapter 5 was published as "The Once and the Now" in
Liberties (Spring 2023).

For Diana Cooper

Artist

It is a common sentence that Knowledge is power;
but who hath duly considered or set forth the
power of Ignorance?

—George Eliot, *Daniel Deronda*

CONTENTS

Ignorance and Bliss

INTRODUCTION

The faintest of all human passions is the love of
truth.

—A. E. Housman

There was a man who lived in a cave. He did not
know that's where he lived, because his legs had been
chained to the ground and his head was enveloped by
a device that projected a virtual life not his own. One
day an unknown woman removed the device and un-
locked the chains, and he saw for the first time where
he and many others actually were. He was shattered.
The woman comforted him as best she could and said
she was there to take him away. As he was preparing
to leave, the man noticed a young boy who had been
sitting next to him, his legs also bound, his small head
invisible inside the grotesque machine. Out of pity he
asked the woman if he could take the boy along. She
agreed, and they departed.

The climb out of the cave was difficult. When they
emerged, the man and boy found themselves in a light
so intense that at first they could hardly open their
eyes. Little by little, as their vision adjusted, they began to see vague forms illuminated by the sun. These
forms, though difficult to describe, were somehow

pleasing. The woman called them Ideas and explained that they, and only they, "truly are," and that all else is illusion. Neither the man nor the boy understood what she was saying, but they found it, too, somehow pleasing. The woman left and did not return for several years.

When she did, she made a request. Now that the man had been freed and lived happily in the light, would he be willing to return to the cave and bring someone else out, just as she had done for him? He agreed and said he would take the boy down with him. But the next morning, after thinking back on the hardships of the first journey, he decided to go alone. He could do the work himself, so why make the boy suffer and deprive him of time in the sun? He called the boy over and announced the good news: he would be staying behind.

The boy began to weep, softly at first, then in earnest. The man was touched by his devotion but told him he should remain in paradise. The boy then fell to his knees and grabbed the man's cloak, pleading, *No, no, you must take me back! I can't live here any longer, I hate it.* The man was stunned. He asked what was wrong, and the boy began to pour out his grievances between sobs:

I'm always cold here. The light is bright, but generates no heat. It reveals everything to my eyes, but doesn't warm my body. It is so strong that all the colors are washed away; the Ideas are like bleached skeletons, like death. I miss shadows, the night sky, the stars, even if they were illusions.

I can't sleep. Back in the cave I would sometimes dream at night of things I'd never seen, imagining myself in unknown places doing unexpected things. Now I no longer dream. I know too much. I know what is and that nothing else can ever be real. Isn't that terrible? How can you stand it?

I'm sad all the time. And I miss my playmates, even if they were just pixels on a screen. Here, no one plays or pretends or even tells a joke. What would be the point? You don't love me, I don't love you: we know too much even for that. I want to go home.

And so he did.

Aristotle taught that *all human beings want to know.* Our own experience teaches us that all human beings also want not to know, sometimes fiercely so. This has always been true, but there are certain historical periods—we are living in one—when the denial of evident truths seems to be gaining the upper hand, as if some psychological bacillus were spreading by unknown means, the antidote suddenly powerless. Mesmerized crowds follow preposterous prophets, irrational rumors trigger fanatical acts, and magical thinking crowds out common sense and expertise. One can always find proximate causes of such surges in resistance to truth, whether historical events or social changes or new intellectual and religious currents promising a holiday from reality. The source lies deeper, though, in ourselves and in the world itself, which takes no heed of our wishes.

The world is a recalcitrant place, and there are things about it we would prefer not to have to recognize. Some are uncomfortable truths about ourselves; those are the hardest to accept. Others are truths about outer reality that, once revealed, steal from us beliefs and feelings that have somehow made our lives better, easier to live—or so we think. The experience of disenchantment is as painful as it is common, and it is not surprising that a verse from an otherwise forgotten English poem became a common proverb: *Ignorance is bliss.*

We can all come up with reasons why we and others avoid knowing particular things, and many of those reasons are perfectly rational. A trapeze artist, just before climbing the pole, would be unwise to consult the actuarial table for those in her line of work; a young poet should pass up the chance of asking an older one what she thinks of his verses. Even the question *Do you love me?* should not trip off our tongues, but rather pass through several checkpoints before being uttered. If we knew what every person thought of us at every moment (imagine a small LED screen embedded in every forehead, relaying every thought), we would not only feel paralyzed before them; we would also have trouble attaining any independent sense of ourselves, free from the opinions of others.

Even self-knowledge, the beginning of wisdom, depends on resisting at least this kind of knowledge about the world.

So in particular cases we all have instrumental reasons for avoiding the truth, the whole truth, and nothing but the truth. Our lives, though, are not made up of a string of discrete, unrelated moments in which we decide to seek knowledge about one thing, then decide not to seek it about another. Life is not an assembly-line job where we are tasked with sorting experiences into one box or another—*want to know, don't want to know*—as they chug down the conveyor belt. We all have a basic disposition toward knowing, a way of carrying ourselves in the world as experiences come our way. Some people just are naturally curious about how things got to be the way they are; they like puzzles, they like to search things out, they enjoy learning *why*. Others are indifferent to learning and see no particular advantage to asking questions that seem unnecessary for just carrying on. And then there are people who, for whatever reason, have developed a particular antipathy toward the search for knowledge, whose inner doors are fastened tight against anything that might cast doubt on what they believe they already know. We have all met people with these basic attitudes. Most of us have also fallen into moods where they emerge in ourselves, however uncharacteristically.

Knowing is an emotional experience. It is not simply a matter of the senses sending messages to the brain, synapses firing, propositions being formed and their logic tested. The desire to know is exactly that, a *desire*. And whenever our desires are satisfied or thwarted, our feelings are engaged. Even in trivial matters, we feel something about what we learn. Say, for example, a toaster I own breaks and needs to be fixed. I look at the manual, I watch videos, I ask questions, I tinker, and with any luck I learn how to make it work again. I feel satisfied, and doubly so. Not only can I use the machine again, I have also confirmed my sense of being the kind of person who can seek knowledge, find it, and use it. Toast and self-satisfaction: not a bad way to start the day.

The extraordinary thing about instrumental curiosity like this, though, is that it can be transformed, seemingly spontaneously, into a more general yearning to understand—a disposition. I set out to discover one fact and become transfixed by another. I wander off the path of my original purpose and soon find myself happily lost. An interest in fixing my toaster has become an interest in how electricity makes it run. I consult websites about engineering, which are linked to other ones about the laws of physics, a more interesting subject than I had expected. And those pages provide useful links to books and documentaries about physicists and their discoveries about the cosmos. Books start arriving in the mail, I stay up late watching the films, though they have nothing to do with my original purpose. Mildly obsessed, I share what I've learned with family and friends, trying their patience. What began as an amusement has become somehow important to me. Something has shifted inside, and my disposition toward life has changed, however narrowly and briefly. The world is no longer simply a means to my ends. It has become an object of puzzlement and wonder. And extraordinary pleasure.

This is a book about the contrary disposition: the will not to know, the will to ignorance.

It was Nietzsche who coined the term, and his description of being in its grip is unforgettable. Opposed to the drive to knowledge, he wrote, is:

> an apparently opposite drive, a suddenly erupting decision in favor of Ignorance, of deliberate exclusion, a shutting of one's windows, an internal No to this or that, a refusal to let things approach, a kind of state of defense against much that is knowable, a satisfaction with the dark, with the limiting horizon, a Yea and Amen to ignorance.

Nietzsche was a hyperbolic thinker and writer, but in this case he was exaggerating nothing. There are people whose disposition toward seeking knowledge can grow weaker or stronger depending on their mood or circumstances. And then there are those whose basic psychological posture, so to speak, is to resist new knowledge. Just as we can develop a love of truth that stirs us within, so we can develop a hatred of truth that fills us with a passionate sense of purpose.

If that seems an alien notion, consider this passage from Pascal's *Pensées* and ask yourself if it doesn't capture a feeling that has welled up within you at some point, or if it is an attitude you have observed in others:

> The self wants to be great, and sees itself small; it wants to be happy, and sees itself wretched; it wants to be perfect, and sees itself full of imperfections; it wants to be the object of men's love and esteem, and it sees that its defects deserve only their dislike and contempt. This embarrassment in which it finds itself produces in it the most unrighteous and criminal passion imaginable, for it conceives a mortal hatred against this truth, admonishing it and convincing it of its faults. It wants to annihilate this truth, but, unable to destroy it in its essence, it destroys it as far as possible in its own knowledge and in that of others.

Resisting knowledge is an emotional experience, too.

Of course, to speak of the mind as being inhabited by *wills* is to speak metaphorically. But we need some sort of term for describing the conflict we experience between the rival emotions generated by our capacity to seek knowledge and to resist it. Living in the shadow of the modern Enlightenment, we are accustomed to hearing curiosity extolled for the material benefits it brings and for the contribution it makes to what we today consider our most precious possession: inner freedom. For just that reason, perhaps, we are less accustomed to observing and reflecting on curiosity as a purely psychological drive charged with unruly passions. There is of course a long tradition of thinking that looks askance at the human passion for knowing and raises doubts about its value for life. Reasons can be given for the desire to know; reasons also can be given for constraining that desire.

But apart from this clash of reasons there is also a clash of unreasoning emotions, with the desire to defend and even cultivate our ignorance standing as a powerful adversary to the desire to escape it. Once one learns to recognize this clash of wills, one begins to see what an important role it plays in our individual and collective lives, and especially in how we think about those lives. As George Eliot put it in the epigraph to this book: *It is a common sentence that Knowledge is power; but who hath duly considered or set forth the power of Ignorance?* That power is what I propose to examine here.

Most writers begin their research with a deflating sense of entering a very crowded field. My experience has been just the opposite: the more I read and thought about the psychology of knowledge-seeking and knowledge-resisting, the more alone I felt. The Western philosophical tradition has a great deal to say about the conditions of acquiring knowledge and whether this is even possible. But despite the axiom that the first step in philosophy is to know the extent of our ignorance, the tradition has astonishingly little to say about acquiring knowledge of our *will* to ignorance. Kant once insightfully remarked that *the ignorant have no concept of their ignorance because they have none of knowledge.* I am tempted to retort that *philosophers have no concept of their knowledge, because they have none of ignorance.* When one turns to the canonical Western philosophers, searching for clues about what it is to live in a state of ignorance and to work to maintain it, there is less of real depth than one has every reason to expect.

In my experience, the deepest treatments of the will to ignorance are to be found in works of the imagination—ancient myths, religious scriptures, epic poetry, plays, and modern novels. This should probably come as no surprise: without the capacity to resist seeing what is right before our eyes, there would be no drama in human life, no movement. A story about someone who discovers that a truth has been kept from him by someone else reveals nothing particularly interesting about what it is to be human (except that some people are liars). A story about someone who has kept the truth from *himself* immediately becomes a work as complex as any watch, with innumerable gears and springs that labor just below the surface of a deceptively lethargic face.

In exposing the ruses of the will to ignorance, literature exposes us to ourselves, which is sufficient for its purposes. What we lack—or at least what I found lacking for my own purposes—is a nonpoetic reflection on the will to ignorance and its polymorphous role in human existence. How is it that we are creatures who want to know *and* not to know? How is it possible for both desires to inhabit the mind? What function does resistance to knowledge serve in shaping our emotions, our self-understanding, and our understanding of the world around us? How has it influenced our common life, our religions, and our cultures? And what does it mean for how we should live? Socrates asserted that *the unexamined life is not worth living for a human being*—from which it does not follow that the relentlessly examined life is. Where does that leave us?

These are only some of the questions that accumulated over the years, and far more quickly than I could adequately deal with them. And so I concluded that perhaps the most useful and stimulating thing I could offer readers would be the vicarious experience of watching someone trying to think through some of them on the page. The book you are about to read is unusual, and I apologize in advance to librarians obliged to catalog it. It can perhaps best be described as an intellectual travelogue retracing my own circuitous and somewhat episodic excursions in reading and thinking about the will not to know. Each chapter is a foray into a particular theme that drew my attention and offered an occasion for reflecting on how that will operates and what happens when it does, not only in individuals but in society and even in history. Within the chapters I have also inserted passages drawn from my reading that serve as a kind of chorus to my thoughts, sometimes supporting, sometimes contradicting, sometimes mocking them. You are being invited on a ramble, not a journey to a fixed destination.

A very quick glance at the terrain before beginning. The book begins with the myth of Oedipus and explores the relation between our intimate struggles with self-knowledge and our unwillingness to seek understanding of the world around us. I then consider the human tendency to transform those inner struggles into religious myths, pitting gods who establish taboos limiting curiosity against humans who heroically, if futilely, rebel against them. The remaining chapters concern fantasies. Beyond its power to inspire resistance to acknowledging reality, the will to ignorance also fuels the imagination and dangles before us illusory alternative realities. One such illusion is that there is a secret, esoteric way of being in the world that gives access to precious hidden truths that are somehow "beyond" reason. Another is the vain hope of preserving our original innocence, or achieving a second one, free from tragic knowledge of human limits, mortality, and evil. Another still is the collective dream of escaping the historical present by returning to an imagined past of bucolic simplicity unburdened by knowledge of the irreversibility of time—or of forcing a leap into a glorious future, where the virtues of times past will be restored. We begin with Oedipus; we end with modern history. As I said, a ramble not a journey.

Throughout, it will be good to bear in mind the story I began with, a parody of Plato's Allegory of the Cave. In Plato's version there is no little boy, there is just the man, who, after being extracted from the cave, redescends to release his former companions and for his troubles is mocked and nearly killed by them. He encounters a powerful resistance to knowing among people unaware of life outside the cave. They do not know what it is like to know. The little boy, on the other hand, does know what knowing is like—*and that is why he wants to escape.* His is a knowing will to ignorance. I imagine him first emerging from the cave baffled and a little scared, but, like all youngsters, intrigued by a new place to explore. I imagine him looking at the Ideas and sometimes enjoying the feeling of having understood. And yet he snaps. The world as it truly is does not welcome him; it looms, oppressively. The price of living this way is too high. He wants to flee and forget what he already knows. He wants a different kind of life from the one that has been thrust upon him. Plato spoke of the *eros* of intellect; the young man is in the grip of the *thanatos* of intellect. If we do not understand both, we do not understand ourselves.

We want to know, we want not to know. We accept truth, we resist truth. Back and forth the mind shuttles, playing badminton with itself. But it doesn't feel like a game. It feels as if our lives are at stake. And they are.

Note to the Reader

In keeping with the informal, exploratory nature of this book, I have not burdened it with elaborate notes referring to scholarly literature. Instead I have appended simple endnotes indicating the source of important quoted passages and offering occasional suggestions for further reading. As for the quotations themselves and the epigraphs sprinkled throughout the book, I have very occasionally trimmed them to highlight the central thought. In the same spirit, passages from the Bible have been drawn from different English translations, most often the King James Version and the Revised Standard Version, depending on the vividness of their expression.

1

The Eyes of Oedipus

ON EVASION

O Oedipus, God help you! God keep you from
the knowledge of who you are!
> —Sophocles, *Oedipus the King*

King Laius of Thebes wanted a son. But the gods,
aware that he once had raped a young boy, would not
have it. The Oracle of Delphi had prophesied that any
son he fathered would murder him and marry the
queen, Jocasta. Terrified, the king kept away from his
young bride. But Jocasta could not accept a celibate
and childless life, so one night she seduced her
drunken husband, and nine months later she bore him
a son. Laius lost no time getting rid of the boy. He
pierced his ankles with a metal rod and gave him to a
servant, with orders that he be exposed in the wild. But
the boy, like many a mythical hero, survived. Shepherds discovered him, and eventually he was brought
to the King of Corinth. The royal couple took him as
their own and named him Oedipus (*swollen foot*).

Oedipus grew up as a prince, expecting to inherit
the kingdom. He never would. One night, a drunkard
in a tavern approached and asked mockingly if he
knew who his real parents were. Rather than dismiss
the poor fool or buy him a drink, Oedipus became
obsessed with this remark. Unable to understand it,
or to forget it, he followed Greek custom and set off
to Delphi to appeal to the Oracle for enlightenment.

There a priestess denied him entrance to the holy temple, claiming that he was unclean because he was destined to murder his father. The terrified Oedipus fled Corinth to escape this fate—which, as we know, is how he came to fulfill it one day. At a country crossroads, jostled by Laius in a passing carriage, Oedipus killed him, unaware of who the old man was.

Oedipus finally made his way to Thebes and, after performing a remarkable feat, unwittingly married his mother, Jocasta. Their reign was long, their children grew, Laius was forgotten. So was the prophecy, until a merciless plague broke out in Thebes years later and his subjects turned to Oedipus for answers. On this occasion he sent a messenger to the Oracle rather than go himself. And as *Oedipus the King* opens, we find this Pandora of the self in his palace, awaiting news from Delphi.

Today Sophocles's play seems less about fate and prophecy than about the vexed problem of self-knowledge—whether it is possible, whether it is in all cases desirable, why we resist it, and how our struggle with it shapes our relation to the world more generally. Oedipus needs knowledge of the world—*what is causing the plague?*—yet he intuits that it may come with poisoned knowledge about himself. As the drama unfolds, we find ourselves asking whether Oedipus already unconsciously possesses what he claims to be seeking. His reaction to the drunkard's remark was so excessive that it must have pointed to something he'd already suspected and feared. Jocasta, too, is playing games. While sharing her son's bed all those years, wouldn't she have noticed his disfigured feet, an unmistakable sign of his identity? Perhaps the house of Oedipus—perhaps all of Thebes—is caught between the will to know and the will not to know the truth about itself.

The Oracle's prophecy arrives: the plague will end only once Laius's murderer is driven out of Thebes. Oedipus seems inexplicably relieved at this news and begins a manic search for the killer. His resistance to the truth about himself is expressed as curiosity about something else, a ruse familiar to psychoanalysts. But he makes the mistake of calling in a famed blind prophet who reveals the reality that Oedipus has been avoiding: *You are the land's pollution*. A confident king would have beheaded the messenger; Oedipus is undone. He doesn't want to believe it, and Jocasta tries to calm him by entering the theater of his self-deception. But every argument she makes against the prophet's revelation only raises doubts in Oedipus's mind, prompting further investigation and further doubt. She pleads with him, *I beg you—do not hunt this thing out—I beg you, if you have any care for your own life*. But he charges ahead. He must have the truth he has spent his whole life fleeing.

And once he does, his first thought is to hunt down Jocasta and kill her, shifting the blame from himself. She, one step ahead of him, commits suicide rather than confront the reality of her marriage. Now alone, Oedipus chooses to blind himself, as if to punish the organs that shattered his self-deception. He never fully acknowledges the horrifying truth—that he desired his mother, possessed her, and enjoyed it.

Carved into the wall of the temple of Delphi was a well-known maxim: *Know thyself.* But farther down the wall was another: *Nothing in excess.* Perhaps this maxim was meant to modify the first.

EVASIVE ACTION

There is no self-knowledge that leaves its object
untouched . . . Nobody remains quite the same
when he knows himself.

—Thomas Mann

Among the recent discoveries of neuroscience is that
radical self-delusion can have an organic source. Doctors have long encountered patients whose capacity for
denial and confabulation was so extraordinary that
they seemed in the grip of pathological certainty, like
Hamlets in reverse. Some suffered from anosognosia,
a neurological disorder that keeps people from recognizing their own physical or mental condition, even
such dramatic ones as partial paralysis. Blind people
who have Anton syndrome are convinced that they
can see, and they speak easily and at length about
whatever visual experience they believe themselves to
be having at any given moment. Korsakoff syndrome
causes people to have false memories that are as real
to them as memories of things that have actually happened. The most terrifying of these conditions is
surely Capgras syndrome, which gives someone the
conviction that his loved ones have been replaced by
imposters. None of these conditions, we now know,

develops solely, if at all, to gratify some deep psychological need or wish. It seems to be in the wiring.

But what about the rest of us? We all suffer from delusions, and we all, like Oedipus, use tricks of self-deception to keep ourselves from acknowledging truths about ourselves. Yet understanding, or even describing, this everyday experience can seem a fool's errand.

Some delusions reflect nothing more than benign self-ignorance. Those who can't hold a tune sing loudest in the choir, and God forgives them in their innocence. Other delusions require active work. We suck in our stomachs when we walk past a shopwindow or elaborately comb our hair to mask encroaching baldness. We do this automatically, though every once in a while we get the mild shock of *catching ourselves* doing it. Our little ruses seem to emerge from a *space between* consciousness and unconsciousness, knowing and not knowing. If, *at some level*, we didn't think we were overweight, we would not have developed the habit of tensing our abdominal muscles; if *a part of us* did not recognize a receding hairline, we would not spend all that time before the mirror. Our mental faculties are not asleep while this is happening, but neither are they giving it their *full attention*. Language fails us the moment we try to put words to what is going on. The phrases I have just italicized— *catching ourselves*, *space between*, *at some level*, *a part of us, full attention*—are feeble and incompatible metaphors we've concocted to make sense of a mystery: that we can be not at one with ourselves, yet somehow still the same. Isn't it strange, a wit once remarked, that Dr. Jekyll and Mr. Hyde both knew the way home?

Perhaps self-evasion is a skill we all should learn. If we could ignore the things about ourselves that keep us from being happy, or "achieving our potential," that might be a good thing. But no religious tradition accepts this view, for very good reasons.

Recall the biblical story of King David and his soldier Uriah the Hittite. One evening, while David's troops were laying siege to a city and he remained in Jerusalem, he saw from his rooftop a beautiful young woman, Uriah's wife, Bathsheba, giving herself a ritual bath. He sent for her, slept with her, and impregnated her. To avoid scandal, he then recalled Uriah from the battlefield and told him to go home and spend the night with his wife, so he might believe that the coming child was his own. But as a matter of honor and out of solidarity with the other troops, Uriah insisted on sleeping outdoors, not with his wife. So the dishonorable David sent him back into battle, giving his generals orders to launch a suicidal assault on the city in hopes that Uriah would be killed. He was. And when the news reached David, he moved Bathsheba into his home and married her.

God was not pleased. But rather than simply punish David, God made him confront himself. He sent to the king the prophet Nathan, who recounted a parable about a rich shepherd who had many sheep, and a poor shepherd who had but one, which *was unto him as a daughter.* One day the rich man stole his neighbor's only lamb to prepare a feast for a visitor rather than sacrifice one of his own large flock. When David heard this story, he forgot that it was a parable and interrupted Nathan, declaring—a little like Oedipus when he received news from Delphi—*As the Lord lives, the man who has done this deserves to die.* And Nathan replied, *You are the man.* David felt the shock of recognition and confessed his hypocrisy. And God accepted his repentence, though his bastard child had to die. That was the price of learning that self-awareness is a necessary condition of moral responsibility, and therefore an obligation.

Yet more seems at stake in self-awareness and self-deception than policing people's behavior toward one another; security cameras can now do that work for us. When we say of someone that *he doesn't know himself* or *he never learns his lesson,* we mean that he unwittingly does harm to himself, not others, and we find this tragic. His suffering has less to do with an external state of affairs than with an internal state of dispossession, with his not being fully at one with himself in his thoughts and actions. We witness him flailing about, we hear his self-reproaches, yet we are unable to relieve his suffering because we cannot provide what he most needs: inner knowledge and recognition of his condition. And there seems to be no way to breach the walls of the unknowing self.

As we learn from Saint Augustine's autobiographical *Confessions*, this was the piteous state of his own soul before his conversion to Christianity. Augustine had grown up in the religious bazaar of late antiquity, where traditional Roman religion, Christianity, and various gnostic and philosophic sects all had adherents. His mother, Monica, was a simple, uneducated Christian woman who conveyed to him all the truths and moral principles he would later propagate as an adult. Yet, as a young man, he resisted them with all his inner strength. Why? A pagan observer at the time might have said it was because Augustine was a healthy young man. He spent his days seeking wisdom wherever he thought he might find it, from rhetoricians, philosophers, even gurus. At night he returned home to enjoy the company of his concubine, with whom he also had a son. The anti-erotic Christianity that Monica professed condemned the vanity of human learning and encouraged chastity. From the pagan standpoint, Augustine had simply chosen the joys of learning and lovemaking over the superstition of the Cross.

But they were not joys to him. In truth, his frantic pursuit of pleasure was a flight from reckoning with a deeper misery and despair that he could not bring himself to acknowledge. It was only when a young friend of his died unexpectedly and he fell into depression that Augustine's latent suffering rose to the surface:

> Everything on which I set my gaze was
> death . . . all that I had shared with my friend
> was without him transformed into a cruel tor-
> ment. My eyes looked for him everywhere,
> and he was not there . . . I had become to my-
> self a vast problem . . . I found myself heavily
> weighed down by a sense of being tired of liv-
> ing and scared of dying . . . Everything was
> an object of horror, even light itself . . . I had
> become to myself a place of unhappiness in
> which I could not bear to be; but I could not
> escape myself.

In this agonized state Augustine had an inkling that
Christianity could help him escape, but something
still kept him from embracing the faith. He described
his then self as being the pawn of two conflicting
wills: one that sought pleasure in sex and vain learning, and another that wanted to rise up to God and be
happy. These were not alien forces that occupied his
soul. They were both, somehow, expressions of the
same self.

Nothing written about the paradox of our not-at-
oneness improves on Augustine's description of it:

> The mind commands the body and is instantly
> obeyed. The mind commands itself and meets
> resistance . . . The mind orders the mind to
> will. The recipient of the order is itself, yet it
> does not perform it . . . We are dealing with a

morbid condition of the mind which, when it is lifted up by the truth, does not unreservedly rise.

And this was precisely his own condition:

> There was a grand struggle in my inner house . . . The self which wished to serve was identical with the self which was unwilling. It was I. I was neither wholly willing nor wholly unwilling. So I was in conflict with myself and was dissociated from myself. And this dissociation came about against my will.

Even his prayers, when he did pray, reflected this state: *Grant me chastity and continence, O Lord, but not yet.* Only after his conversion could he relish the irony.

Confessions reads like a drawn-out game of peek-aboo, with the seeker and sought being Augustine himself. He cannot reach out to God until he stops evading himself, but, like Oedipus, he's incapable of that. And so God in his grace reached out to him. It happened one afternoon while Augustine was listening to a young man recount his own conversion.

> While he was speaking, Lord, you turned my attention back to myself. You took me up from behind my own back where I had placed myself because I did not wish to observe myself, and

you set me before my face so that I should see how vile I was, how twisted and filthy, covered in sores and ulcers. And I looked and was appalled, but there was no way of escaping from myself. If I tried to avert my gaze from myself, his story continued relentlessly, and you once again placed me in front of myself; you thrust me before my own eyes so that I should discover my iniquity and hate it. I had known it, but deceived myself, refused to admit it, and pushed it out of my mind.

You took me up from behind my own back. Of all the metaphors of self-evasion and self-confrontation, it is hard to think of one more vivid than this. Augustine asks us to imagine a Janus-faced self: a conscious one with eyes looking in one direction, with an un-avowed one laminated to its back, looking behind. Other people can see that Augustine is self-divided, but he cannot; he is not blind, yet he cannot see his own misery. And so it takes a divine force to reveal him to himself. God peels off Augustine's unacknowl-edged side, the one that suffers because he wallows in sin, and simply places it before his conscious eyes: *Know thyself.* That is all. No thunderclaps. No falling from horses. No rebirth. No vision of the Kingdom to come. His was a thoroughly human epiphany.

JAILBREAK

In the fight between yourself and the world, bet
on the world.

—Franz Kafka

Today's evangelical churches and Pentecostal movements promote a Happy Meal version of Christian
conversion that promises a *new self* rather than
knowledge of the selves we are each saddled with. After all, didn't Saint Paul declare, *If any man be in
Christ, he is a new creature: old things are passed
away; behold, all things are become new*? The fantasy
is that we can wipe the psychological slate clean and
start over; the reality is that such superficial converts
learn to sweep things under the rug and become even
greater mysteries to themselves. Augustine preached a
confrontation with the self, not an escape from it, and
in *Confessions* invited readers to overcome their own
resistance to seeing the reality of their condition,
which is that they live in an unhappiness whose only
remedy is God's grace. That self-seeing may begin as
an epiphany but then must become an activity that
Christians undertake their entire lives, examining
their souls and avowing the sin they find there. This

labor and divine grace are the necessary, if insufficient, conditions of human happiness.

Freud did not reveal anything about the psychological cost of human self-evasion that Augustine hadn't already known and also experienced. They both saw us inhabiting a world where God seems absent, where we and everyone else are driven by unruly desires that churn our souls and set us at cross-purposes. And they both understood that we work to ignore this fact and the unhappiness it brings. The less we understand our condition, the more we suffer; the more we suffer, the harder we work to evade recognizing our condition. Augustine pointed to himself, Freud pointed to Oedipus, and they saw the same thing: creatures who most fear what they most need.

Freud did not believe in divine grace, of course, and the concept of sin as the ultimate source of our not-at-oneness was alien to him. Instead he preached what is perhaps an even harder doctrine than Augustine's: that our not-at-oneness is actually necessary for human life. It is the source of our pain, but it also protects us from ourselves, allows us to navigate a world we share with others, and is even the source of our achievements. To know oneself is to know that one will never fully know oneself—and that this is a good thing, too.

The drama begins in infancy, when I first encounter the world's recalcitrance. At a certain age I become aware that others are not furniture decorating my rooms, or servants born to oblige, that they have their own desires and the power to thwart mine. This fact comes as a shock. It is unreasonable, it enrages me and causes such pain that unless I ease it as Oedipus did—by committing whatever unclean or murderous act would allow me to have my way—I instinctively try to avoid feeling it. And so I begin to play hide-and-seek with my desires that clash with those of others and with the taboos society imposes to keep us from each other's throats. My drives are still there (wherever *there* is), yet an unconscious will to ignorance helps me to cloak them from consciousness—though they reemerge at night in the Kabuki theater of my dreams, costumed and making inscrutable movements, never removing their masks. When the curtain falls, they disappear and, at least consciously, I feel safe again. Unconsciously, well, that's another matter.

At a certain point I learn a strategy for easing somewhat this inner labor. I succumb to Stockholm syndrome, counterintuitively adopting society's chafing strictures as my own. As a young man, I want sex but am frustrated by the taboos that stand in my way. I struggle to ignore my desires but still experience frustration unconsciously and feel I'm being held prisoner, powerless. Eventually the frustration becomes unbearable; so, like many victims of kidnapping, I begin to side with my jailers and adopt their point of view. I even become their spokesman, defending the reasonableness of their demands before the assembled press. (This, no doubt, would have been Freud's assessment of Saint Augustine.) Now I am no longer powerless. I exercise some control over my destiny, or so I imagine. This is, of course, an illusion: the taboos are externally imposed. But unless I maintain the illusion that I have chosen them, I will be paralyzed by frustration and unable to function in society. And so I build defenses around my illusion and resist any attempt by others to expose it. I take one further, and quite large, step away from self-knowledge, put on a smile, and say in all sincerity, *I'm fine, just fine. Why do you ask?*

This is the Freudian mythos stripped of Freudian technical language. As I say, it is a hard teaching, which makes one suspect it is close to the truth. Coming into a ready-made world, I have no choice but to fit myself into it. And no society, unless it puts police officers in every room, can survive unless the codes that allow it to function are internalized by each individual. That entails loss, including the loss of self-transparency and self-knowledge. But through this loss I also become myself—not just *a* self with desires coursing through it, but my *very* self, an integrated and self-conscious, if not fully self-aware, subject in a world with others. We must all learn this beneficent art of psychological trompe l'oeil. Memories must be stitched together, beliefs that don't fit must be discarded, and any remaining gaps must be filled in. I need to work at self-integration—recognizing some things, ignoring others—just to get through the day and think about tomorrow. I also need to do it if I am to act as a responsible moral agent, which for Freud was the crowning achievement of psychological health. I can never fully know all the conscious and unconscious motives that contribute to my decision, say, to keep a found wallet or return it to its owner. Ethical action, as opposed to mere ethical intention, requires some degree of self-mastery. But it also requires a *sense* of self-mastery, a false belief that I am fully and solely the author of my actions. No self-deception, no morality.

If there is a danger in self-integration, it is that we will overdo it. Integrity is a virtue, but it can make the self as fragile as porcelain, incapable of absorbing anything that deviates from the expected. I am happily married, but I just had an affair with my best friend's husband. I am a colonel, but I am frightened walking down stairs. I am a mother, but I sometimes wish my child were dead. When these discordant thoughts, feelings, and actions surge up, the mechanisms of repression and resistance are set in motion. They may succeed in keeping me together for a time. But the more such things accumulate, the more the inner pressure accumulates and causes me pain. To relieve it, all I can do is work harder to delude myself about the gap between the way I and society agree I should feel, and the way I actually do feel. And the longer I practice extreme self-deception, the more toxic the truth about myself becomes to me. Like Oedipus, I must avoid it at all costs. I am no longer just a question to myself, I have become alien to myself. I long for escape.

Neuroses are jailbreaks—not out of a prison but into one. *Today neurosis takes the place of the monasteries*, Freud wrote, *which used to be the refuge of all whom life had disappointed or who felt too weak to face it.* The monastery simile was well chosen and has a contemporary ring. Today we are becoming aware of just how many Catholic priests have sought refuge from unavowable same-sex desires by retreating into a community where such desires were both condemned and satisfied. This is how Freud saw many of his straightlaced Viennese patients, as suffering from too much rigid integration and retreating into neurotic symptoms to escape themselves. What they needed was to learn how to recognize and accept their own inner complexity. But how to reach them once they had retreated into their cells and locked the doors from within?

In the popular imagination even today, psychoanalysis is thought to offer a transformative eureka moment that unveils *the source of the problem* and thereby magically dissolves it. A patient is miserable, but does not know why. He consults an analyst, who listens to him talk about his problems and feelings and asks probing questions. Through this back-and-forth the analyst gets a better picture of the patient's psychological makeup, enabling her to develop a diagnosis based on scientific training. Once the diagnosis is made, it is delivered to the patient like a writ of habeas corpus, releasing him from his delusions. But if all that was required to relieve psychological suffering was knowledge of the self, and if that could be acquired simply by mastering psychological science, then reading books or listening to lectures about it would offer as much relief as treatment by an analyst. But this doesn't work. Freud's experience with patients taught him that mere insight into the conscious and unconscious mind *has as much influence on the symptoms of nervous illness as a distribution of menu-cards in a time of famine has upon hunger.*

What the popular view of psychoanalysis fails to appreciate is the power and wiliness of resistance. The person who locks himself in prison to evade knowledge of himself has done so for a reason, and he stays there out of fear of what lies outside. He would be a fool to come out just because someone on the other side of the door sounded the all clear. Even if that someone were to slip an envelope under the door with a note explaining how the prisoner mistakenly got to be there, and even if the envelope contained photos of things that confirmed the note's contents, he still would ignore it. Who says the writer is to be trusted?

And trust is exactly what suffering patients lack. They cannot believe that the revelation of a truth about themselves won't bring the world crashing down around them. That is why they resist treatment and their therapists. In the early years of psychoanalysis Freud ignored this dimension and felt that his patients' evident feelings for him, whether positive or negative, just got in the way of his work. Then he realized that their emotional investment in him provided an opening. He noticed during sessions that a patient's resistance to recognizing his own problematic relation to himself was being transferred over to his relationship with the analyst; what was going on inside the self was being reproduced in the consulting room. Freud surmised that if this resistance to the therapist could be diminished by building trust through the activity of conversation, then the patient's resistance to avowing some aspects of himself would also decrease. If he experienced a safe search for the truth about himself with a trustworthy companion, he might find it easier to confront himself in life after therapy. Truth would be detoxified.

Freud believed that we need a great deal of actual knowledge of ourselves, once it has been made palatable, to lead an autonomous life. Just repairing the web of our beneficent self-evasions is not sufficient and invites a regression. It is an illusion to think that this knowledge or self-mastery could ever be complete, though. We are necessarily mysteries to ourselves, and any notion that we can become fully at one, once and for all, is a fantasy akin to the suburban ideal of the perfectly manicured lawn. Anything we achieve in the search for self-understanding must be gotten through work; it entails sweat and strain and moments of despair. And it never ends. There is no one out there with a magic hand to peel our second selves off our backs for us. The most we can hope to achieve, compared with the false promise of epiphanic conversion, is modest: an ability to live within the limits of what we are and all that any society can provide, freedom from pointless guilt, sexual enjoyment, moral responsibility, and a capacity to develop ourselves without aggression or self-cruelty. That is all. Freud thought it was sufficient.

He also thought that achieving such a state would permit us to turn our attention away from ourselves and toward the wondrous world around us. In the last decade of his life he took some solace in the hope that some of the repressed energy of our drives could be sublimated and diverted in socially useful ways. He spoke of artists who take the crude oil of desire and spin it into gossamer, giving themselves and their audience a higher and more lasting pleasure. He spoke of the rare souls whose gifts permit them to expend their diverted energies in the pursuit of scientific truth, and was pleased to include himself in this group. He did not think science could unveil all the secrets of nature, or even of the psyche. But he did believe that whatever was discovered through scientific methods was solid, reliable. Human beings were learning that the reward of science was a tentative but increasingly secure knowledge of nature and the basic conditions of life, including psychological life. And that this knowledge could be acquired by ourselves, without appeal to gods or spirits or aliens. To accept knowledge of our limitations and our desires is difficult. But to receive in recompense knowledge of the world itself—who could resist that?

Answer: just about everyone.

ZIPPERS

A man walking through a village saw a donkey braying at a dog, who was barking back at the donkey. Astonishingly, as the man approached them he began to understand their conversation. *Grass and pastures, that's all you talk about,* complained the dog. *What really matters are rabbits and cow bones, nothing else.*

Unable to restrain himself, the man interjected, *But it is grass that feeds the rabbits and cows.* In a flash, the two animals turned on him. After they had driven him away, they continued their argument.

—Sufi story

At every age we find reasons not to think. Not just about ourselves and what we really are, but about the world and how it really is. It is one thing to resist toxic knowledge of the inner self, as Oedipus and Augustine did. It is another thing, initially more puzzling, to resist knowledge of abstract truths or external reality, which can help us navigate the world and reach our own ends. But we do resist, often with equal vigor. And there is a reason for that: the less the knower knows himself, the less he knows what it is to have knowledge of anything and the limits of that knowledge. Evasion of the self inside our heads is really a training exercise for evading the world outside our heads.

Consider Cephalus, a wealthy Athenian gentleman who lived near the Greek port of Piraeus, just down the hill from the city. One day Socrates paid him a visit and found him in the kind of "philosophical" mood that old rich men at their leisure tend to get into. Cephalus was eager to tell Socrates that he'd discovered the secret to a happy life. Having been freed from the passions of youth, especially erotic ones, he now saw that genuine happiness does not depend on satisfying desires, it depends on character and good cheer instead. As for money, only the just man really benefits from it, while it makes the unjust man more vicious and miserable. Ethics first, then grub.

Socrates seemed impressed by this proclamation, which has much to recommend it. But he also sensed that Cephalus had never inquired seriously about these matters or about himself and had only contracted a late case of piety. So he asked him a simple question: What do you mean by the term *just*? Cephalus was caught up short. Men of his age and standing are not in the habit of being examined, but they are experienced enough to sense a potential threat, no matter how politely put. So rather than answer Socrates's question, he graciously excused himself and went to make sacrifices to the gods, turning the conversation over to his excitable, thickheaded son.

A great and instructive pleasure in reading Plato's dialogues is witnessing what happens when a seemingly disembodied argument is expressed by a flesh-and-blood human being who has feelings and passions, in front of other human beings who have their own. Time and again we are reminded that arguments are not always transparent, that there can be a gap between what people in the heat of argument say they believe and what their behavior in the conversation reveals. Socrates's philosophical concern is not only to find the truth about whatever he and his friends happen to be discussing. He also appears eager to understand people's emotional response to the quest, and, in particular, how and why anyone would resist learning what is true.

Conversations with Socrates have a predictable arc. They begin with pleasantries, then get difficult and sometimes very technical. And then, very often, something goes awry. The conversation hits a thick wall, and no further advance seems possible. Other times a conversation with one of the speakers disintegrates when it runs into bad psychological weather. Something Socrates says sets off sirens and flashing lights, and the speaker flees, or turns on him. We've all had this experience in our everyday conversations. A discussion begins, and we feel ourselves in a partnership with the person we're speaking with.

Égalité et fraternité. Then something happens, a word or phrase or change in tone ruins the mood, and one of us gets frustrated or offended. We find an excuse to leave. Or we stay, and now the conversation is no longer about the matter at hand, but about the two of us. The contest for command begins, trenches are dug, barbed wire laid, mortars stockpiled. *Victoria o muerte.*

In Socrates we witness a new way of doing philosophy that makes inquiry into the world dependent on inquiry into the self and its capacity for knowledge. But we also witness an afterbirth—anti-philosophical anger. Socrates pretended to be perplexed by the hatred caused by his activity, which was to wander around the city and engage people in conversation. No one was ever compelled to join these discussions, though sometimes Socrates had to be nudged. And all he tried to convey to people, he claimed, was that learning the truth, even about themselves, is always to their advantage. We should want to question our beliefs and the justice of our actions, he tells them, so we can improve our souls and be truly happy. We shouldn't fear learning the truth, even about death, since it is meaningless to one who has lived well; if we haven't lived well, then vice, not death, is our problem. Above all, we shouldn't get angry with someone who points out contradictions in our thinking or refutes our arguments, especially when they concern the most important question, which is how to live. No one ever loses a truly philosophical argument: this was Socrates's most radical teaching.

Plato's dialogues show just how hard it is to accept such a teaching. Time and again we see that the inner citadels of Socrates's interlocutors are guarded by a corps of resistances, and that no good argument can pass through unless the guards are disarmed or lulled to sleep. The most obvious resistance is rooted in fear. Socrates's conversations almost always wend their way into sensitive territory, where people's beliefs about ultimate things—morality, religion, mortality— come into question and they feel exposed. By questioning those beliefs, people risk upsetting ideas they've built their lives around, with no guarantee of finding satisfying new ones. We may think we're brave enough for that, but how many of us are? Atheists who take comfort in a comfortless world would find it very uncomfortable to discover that the God of the Bible does, in fact, exist. Their little inner world would collapse.

If the search for truth were to take place in a state of total ignorance, there would be no reason or occasion to resist. That is not our case. Instead, almost all inquiry begins with received false opinions in which people have an emotional stake. That is why the philosopher must also be a psychologist when pursuing arguments with others, or even with himself. Socrates sometimes calls himself a midwife, a perfect metaphor for his craft. The people he speaks with bring to the conversation distinct emotions concerning their beliefs. Were the truth to be dumped on them, they would be incapable of digesting it and would reject it. And so it must be coaxed out of them in ways that are in accord with what they already are and how they think, and that avoid particular resistances. The contracted muscles that maintain ignorance must be relaxed.

No one can hold an opinion for us. It is ours—or, better put, it is an extension of our very self, a prosthetic device. When it is attacked or dismissed, we feel that something intimate has been touched. And when it fails, we feel ashamed. Socrates maintained that there is no shame in being wrong, just in doing wrong. He was right. But it's not the way we initially feel, especially when someone else exposes our errors.

No argument is disembodied. Behind every assertion there is an assertor, and it is he, not his assertion, who wounds our pride. That is why serious conversations even among friends can go so wrong so fast. And it doesn't matter what the subject is. Freud, whose science was all about the building and overcoming of resistance, was notorious for his unwillingness to accept criticism or emendation (and for revising his theories in light of criticism without acknowledging his critics). Mathematicians and scientists debating matters at the furthest remove from daily life can be as dogmatic, partisan, and touchy as any xenophobe. A new boson has been discovered: Is that one giant leap for mankind or one point for our side? Socrates held that the spirit of philosophy, the love of wisdom (*philo-sophia*), was diametrically opposed to the spirit of combat, the love of victory (*philo-nikia*). Yet both spirits get activated when we engage in argument. That there is an International Mathematical Olympiad for national teams of young people tells us a lot about the human animal.

But there was something about Socrates and his manner that was particularly maddening to the Athenians. It had to do with the fact that he so often practiced his medicine in public, not in private, as physicians do. This ultimately sealed his fate in the eyes of his future Athenian murderers. Most of his conversations took place before an audience that he and his interlocutor were aware of, and which the reader must bear in mind. To be refuted by Socrates was a public humiliation, despite his insistence that there was no shame in it.

And Athens at the time was a democracy. Though ancient democracies were very different from our own, the psychology of democratic citizens has not changed. The fundamental article of democratic faith is that people are equal and that they know, individually and collectively, what's best for them. Democrats are tetchy. As Socrates tells one young man, Athenians don't mind your being clever; what they mind is your presuming to teach them and others what you've learned. Many Athenians were offended even when he simply asked questions, and perhaps rightly so. There was something coy about Socrates's irony that gave the impression he was stringing you along, not taking you seriously as an equal—an important thing to democratic citizens. The rules of the road stipulate that everyone gets his say without fear of interrogation. That's what freedom means to Athens. Inquiry into the truth is what freedom means to Socrates.

At one point he took a little tour around the city, trying to ascertain exactly who knew what. He talked to craftsmen who knew their craft but believed that their knowledge applied to every area of life. He spoke with poets who had flashes of insight, but could not explain why what they saw was true. And he spoke in public with a famous, unnamed politician and showed to all assembled that this man knew the least. After that, Socrates told the jury at his trial, *I became hateful to him and to many of those present.* There is a large lesson in those italicized words. Even spectators who had not been humiliated turned against the man who asked too many questions. He had broken the social contract.

Athens, *c'est nous.* At some point we all decline the invitation Socrates makes to us to learn what really is the case. We willingly give up a shot to acquire true beliefs about the world out of fear that truths about ourselves will be exposed in the process, especially our insufficient courage for self-examination. We prefer the illusion of self-reliance and embrace our ignorance for no other reason than it is ours. It doesn't matter that reliance on false opinion is the worse sort of dependence. It doesn't matter that through stubbornness we might pass up a chance at happiness. We prefer to go down with the ship rather than have our names scraped off its hull. Socrates says he doesn't understand why anyone would get angry at someone who wants to help him. He's right, it makes no sense. But every child wants to zip his own coat.

BARSTOOLS

Disillusion as the last illusion.

—Wallace Stevens

At the back of the classroom, or two stools down the bar, you'll find him—the man with the X-ray eyes. He sees through it all. Whatever subject you discuss, he recites the same catechism: noble actions always have selfish motives, institutions only serve those who run them, beliefs are manufactured to oppress, and every book, every idea, every artwork, every utterance expresses a hidden agenda. Nothing is what it seems. This is the esoteric wisdom that joins in intellectual matrimony the sophomore smart aleck and the college professor whose vanity is fed every semester by revealing the truth that truth is an illusion and that everything is permitted. (Which his students, a step ahead of him, take to mean that nothing is worth doing.)

The art of rising from high to low is not difficult to learn. But why do people feel compelled to master it? To turn the tables, what's *behind* their belief that all is illusion? What *function* does it serve? For the simple-minded, it offers a way of appearing thoughtful without expending effort. If all politicians are liars, there is no reason to take politics seriously or learn anything about it; if standards of morality are arbitrary, there is no need to look in the mirror and question yourself. Why genuinely reflective people adopt this pose is more of a mystery. They are not practitioners of Nietzsche's *gaya scienza*, leaping from joy to joy once freed from the cage of convention. They are angry, and they want you to share their anger; nothing matters more to them than proving to you that nothing can be proved to be true. It's as if they've suffered some sort of trauma they can forget only by embracing the void and inviting company, a prospect that frightens them less than . . . what exactly?

Socrates coined a word for some such people: he called them *misologues*, haters of argument. Misology, he explained, comes about the same way that misanthropy does:

> Hatred of argument and hatred of human beings come about in the same way. For hatred of human beings arises from artlessly trusting someone to excess, and believing that human being to be in every way true and sound and trustworthy, and then a little later discovering that this person is wicked and untrustworthy— and then having this experience again with another . . . [It is similar] when somebody trusts some argument to be true without the art of arguments, and then a little later the argument seems to him to be false and this

happens again and again with one argument after another. Those especially who've spent their days in debates end up thinking they've become the wisest of men and that they alone have detected that there's nothing sound or stable.

Socrates spoke from some experience. As a young man, he was curious about nature, wanting to understand everything about it. How do things come to be, and why do they perish? Does thought arise from body, or is mind an independent entity? How does one become two? Someone suggested that he consult the works of the philosopher Anaxagoras, who supposedly proved that *Mind is the cause of all things*. Socrates found this idea congenial and thought he'd found his master. But the more he read Anaxagoras, the more confused the older philosopher appeared; no sooner did he start talking about Mind than he lost his way, babbling about things he clearly knew nothing about. Socrates felt betrayed. Clearly there was something wrong, not just with Anaxagoras's system, but with his manner of inquiry. And perhaps not just his. Maybe philosophy itself was pointless, and philosophers nothing but poseurs.

This is how misology begins. The misologue is not indifferent to truth; though he cannot avow it, he loves and wants to know what truly is. But he is overeager, unable to deal with disappointment. Our desire for truth is an *eros*, subject to the same vicissitudes as our *eros* for sexual pleasure. There are lovers who maintain a sense of proportion when they are spurned or after an affair ends, and there are lovers who withdraw and become hermits, cursing the very idea of love and warning anyone who will listen against it. Their pride is wounded because they've chosen badly. But rather than learn from the mistake, they comfort themselves with having seen through the illusion quicker than most.

Misologues make a similar mistake, but with arguments rather than people. At first they put their faith in one argument, then another, without stepping back to consider what arguments can and can't do for them. Nor—since there's no assertion without an assertor—do they consider the nature of the people who use and misuse them. They don't see that just as there's an art of judging people, so there's an art of judging arguments—and, by extension, an art of knowing and judging oneself. Without these arts, misologues and misanthropes eventually kill their *eros* and build walls against its rebirth. What began as a search for knowledge about the world turns into an evasion of the self and its failures.

A Greek rhetorician named Thrasymachus is a good example of this type. Plato made him a character in *The Republic* to illustrate how difficult it is to break through the defenses of someone whose search for truth has gone badly. When Thrasymachus first speaks, we discover that he has been sitting in the room all along while the others were discussing justice. But the more he listened to Socrates, the angrier he got, to the point where he had to be restrained by others in the room. Eventually he lunged at Socrates, accusing him of toying with his audience and not saying what he truly believes. You believe, he said, what all grown-ups know: that justice is nothing but *what benefits the stronger*—nothing more, nothing less. Then he sat back with a triumphant smile.

Misologues are like that. They like to have their cynical say, they like the verbal *geste*. What they don't like is the unpredictability of philosophical dialogue, which is conducted by means of questions and responses, not one-sided assertions. To commit to dialogue is to commit yourself to possible exposure as mistaken or foolish or dogmatic, and misologues would let the cup of this self-knowledge pass them by. They have been wounded enough by asking too many questions.

But Socrates won't let Thrasymachus go. He wants to understand why discussing justice makes Thrasymachus so angry, and he begins to question him about his pat formula. Does it mean that the strong are actually justified in dominating the weak—that might actually does make right? If so, then we don't need the word *right* at all, just *might*. Or does it mean that *justice* is a meaningless term invented by the powerful to exploit the weak? If so, then why get angry? If there's no such thing as justice, there's no such thing as injustice either. Or does Thrasymachus mean what many of us mean when we encounter injustices in the world—that "might" *unjustly* makes "right" to suit itself? That is a very good reason to get angry, though not at Socrates.

And that seems to be Thrasymachus's reason, too, though he lacks the self-awareness to see it. He clearly doesn't understand why he's so angry. But the more he speaks, the more he reveals himself to be a lover of justice who can no longer bear the fact that the righteous suffer and the wicked prosper. He's angry that the truth about justice is impotent in the face of injustice. And he's angry that no one sees what he sees, that all common pieties about justice are intellectually indefensible and mask the vile reality. And Socrates is complicit in this, he believes. Socrates pretends not to know that just as shepherds raise their sheep only to slaughter them, rulers only rule their subjects to fleece them. And to think that we ourselves behave justly for any other reason than fear of punishment is absurd; if we could make ourselves invisible and get away with injustice, we would. Look around, and you see that the strong are mightier, freer, and more masterful than the weak. So why be a sucker? Why not throw our lot in with them?

Thrasymachus has snapped. We all know people like him. They like telling their own conversion stories: I once was naïve about the world, but after *X*— the last election, the recent war, the endless scandals, the world's indifference, fake news—I got wise. And

you can, too. (Misologues hate to be alone.) Dostoyevsky understood this psychological state better than
anyone. In so many of his novels we meet seemingly
wicked characters who are really only in despair, their
original goodness having been robbed by someone or
by circumstances beyond their control. And to cope
with the trauma, they convince themselves that there
is no such thing as goodness, becoming prostitutes or
rakes or drunkards or revolutionaries, reveling in their
baseness. But then they are undone when they meet
genuinely good people and grow to hate them. They
lash out to defend their picture of the world. Goodness must die if their view of the world is to survive.

Thrasymachus cannot bear the gap between what
is and what should be. And because he cannot find a
way through reason to defend justice in the face of this
reality, he turns against reason itself. He no longer
wants the truth he once wanted, and would spurn it if
he found it. Only victory will slake his anger. After
being refuted, Thrasymachus blushes and falls silent
for a time, and Socrates has acquired yet another enemy. This is the tragedy of misology: it transforms potential lovers of knowledge—about themselves and the
world—into enemies of reason. Thrasymachus might
have been Socrates's comrade, but he lacked the courage to persist in the face of disappointment. His will
to knowledge had, thanks to anger, metamorphosized
into a stubborn will to ignorance. Now he's a lost soul
and has embraced his lostness. Like Oedipus, he blinds
himself.

2

Veils

ON TABOO

Too much truth confounds us.

—Pascal

The roof that keeps out the rain also blocks out the sun.

—André Gide, *Paludes*

In Friedrich Schiller's poem "The Veil of Isis," a young European traveler arrives at a temple door in Egypt, demanding to be let in. His eyes are wild, and the priest has trouble making out what he is saying. It seems he has traveled many months to this town in the Nile Delta to be in the presence of the goddess Isis and learn Truth from her. Not particular truths about the nature of the cosmos, say, or the best way to live. He wants Truth itself, whatever that is. *What do I have when I don't have it all? Isn't your truth one and indivisible? Take one note from a chord, take one color from the rainbow, and what remains is nothing.* The priest sighs. *That*, he says, *you must settle with the Goddess.*

The heavy door opens and the pair stroll into the rotunda, which is dominated by the formidable marble statue. The face of Isis is veiled. The visitor cannot hide his disappointment and asks the priest if he has ever peered behind it, or been tempted to. *Never*, the old man says, his eyes widening. *The Goddess has laid down a curse:*

"No mortal hand," said she,
"May lift this veil till I myself shall lift it.
But he whose sacrilegious guilty hand
Will grasp at this forbidden sacred veil,
He"—says the Goddess—"will look on Truth."

The young man tosses and turns in his narrow bed that night, unable to sleep. Eventually, and almost mechanically, he rises, goes to the temple, scales the wall, and enters the rotunda, his steps echoing in the moonlit interior. He hears an inner voice ask if he really intends to tempt the Holy of Holies, and hesitates for a moment. Then he hears his own voice calling out, *Be what it may behind, I lift it now!*

The temple priests find him the next morning, crumpled and unconscious before the statue. He survives, but his life is joyless from that moment on. He would never speak about what he had seen—for what could he say? Who would believe him that the cruelest punishment for curiosity is sometimes the truth, the whole truth, and nothing but the truth? Who, that is, except Oedipus?

THE CABINET OF DR. SALAZAR

Though the 36-year rule of Portugal's
dictator António de Oliveira Salazar ended
last year, the old man is not yet aware of it.
Still immobilized after a stroke and a coma
13 months ago, Salazar calls Cabinet meetings,
and his old ministers faithfully attend—even
though some of them are no longer in the
Cabinet. No one has found the courage to tell
the 80-year-old dictator that he has been
replaced.

> —*Time* magazine (October 31, 1969)

Oedipus was the tragic victim of his own will to ignorance. But it is hard to imagine a non-tragic life for
ourselves without this inner capacity to forestall
knowledge. In truth, we veil ourselves all the time, for
reasons having nothing to do with incest or the enigmatic warnings of mysterious statues. At its most benign, putting limits on our curiosity can be a kind of
game we play with ourselves. We have all planned surprise parties and are delighted when they are thrown
for us, complete with presents that are wrapped to
pique our curiosity. We also enjoy certain kinds of sus-

pense and even try to build it up artificially. When friends begin recounting the plot of a movie they have just seen, but we haven't, we hold up our palms as if they were stop signs so they don't spoil things. And of course couples routinely ask doctors not to show them ultrasound images revealing the sex of their unborn children, so they can experience another kind of suspense on the day of birth. None of this is strictly necessary, but it does somehow add sweetness to life. And no one finds it objectionable or fraught.

In other areas of life, though, veils are required to protect those we love from knowing things that might inadvertently harm them. Discretion is essential in human relations, especially erotic ones. How many couples have foundered when one of them asks and the other one shares a little too much about the past? This should be obvious, and perhaps once was. But discretion is a hard sell in democratic societies that value openness and transparency. After visiting the United States in the early nineteenth century, Alexis de Tocqueville remarked that American parents and children seemed much more like friends when compared with hierarchical French families. He found the intimacy refreshing. Whenever I teach his *Democracy in America*, I ask students whether they think of their parents as friends, and in one class the reaction to the idea was particularly negative. I then learned that most of the students came from families of divorce, and many felt that one parent had become too dependent on them, oversharing, as they put it. *I want my mom to be my mom*, one frustrated young woman said. *I don't want to hear how her date went.*

Certain social customs also act as beneficent veils by limiting our ability to pry too deeply into the lives of others. Requiring uniforms in certain contexts is an example. It used to be more common for people in particular jobs and professions to have a separate set of clothing associated with their work, which they would don before starting their shift at the hospital or joining the assembly line or taking the first food order of the day. Some now consider such costumes demeaning, especially those associated with low-status or dirty work, on the grounds that they imply that the worker is an inferior. Such people, I'm guessing, have never held such jobs. The reverse is probably closer to the truth: I may be a sanitation worker when I wear these overalls, but the moment I remove them, I become a private citizen like everyone else. If I wear the same type of clothing off the job and on, I have a harder time compartmentalizing aspects of my own life and signaling to you that my job does not define me. Overalls protect my dignity.

There also is a social interest in veiling brutal activities to protect the public's moral sensibilities from being coarsened by exposure to them, though we are less explicit about this now than formerly. Thankfully, we no longer execute criminals in public, and even when we did, hangmen and executioners who carried out death sentences were usually masked, so that those watching would not associate the act with a particular person. The aim was to turn the hooded figure into a symbol of impersonal laws or the will of the sovereign. Slaughterhouses and food processing plants are still generally kept out of sight, not only to conceal the stench and the pollution they cause, but to keep the public from becoming habituated to the sight and sounds of killings. Political activists are understandably suspicious of any talk of benevolent veiling when it comes to these cases. Hoping that a confrontation with unfiltered reality will change the public's feelings and behavior, animal rights groups make documentaries about the cruelties we commit in order to eat meat. Antiabortion activists do the same with photographic images of fetuses in the womb. But as we have learned from live press coverage of war and videos of terrorist killings, unfiltered exposure to death can have the opposite effect, habituating and desensitizing us to it. The taboo against vivisection stood in the way of medical progress for centuries, and we are well rid of it. Still, it must to be admitted that the ban reinforced a sense of the mystery and sacredness of life that we have trouble maintaining. We still don't live-stream autopsies, though how long this will be taboo is anyone's guess.

Even democratic institutions must observe limits to openness and transparency if they are to treat people justly. Voting needs to be anonymous, and jurors are expected to render judgment based solely on the evidence presented to them, not on what they run across on the internet. In some democratic countries there are also strong journalistic norms against publishing the names and photos of those arrested for crimes until they have been formally charged. This has never been so in the United States, where the perp walk, in which someone recently arrested is paraded before the cameras in handcuffs, is regularly performed. This experience can scar a young person for life and also stand in the way of a convicted criminal's eventual reinsertion into democratic society. The psycho-dynamics of forgiveness and rehabilitation depend on our ability to shift our attention from the past, hiding it somewhere behind a veil in the mind. If the past is fully and vividly accessible 24/7, we break the implicit contract behind all criminal justice: that one can *pay for one's crimes*, *move on*, *start over*, *turn over a new leaf*—many metaphors for a pressing human and so-cial need. One can understand why a number of coun-tries have passed laws establishing a right to be forgotten on the internet.

> Something there is that doesn't love a wall . . .
> —Robert Frost, "Mending Wall"

And so, yes, it is sometimes wise, and sometimes even enjoyable, to place a veil before our own eyes. Why is it, then, that the moment we encounter limits to our curiosity, something in us rebels and wants to transgress them—without an inkling of what's being kept from us and despite the likelihood that it might do us harm. The Romans coined the term *curiositas* to describe exactly this irrational impulse to bang on a locked door, just because it is locked, and to sneak through the window if we are not admitted. Busybodies who rudely intrude in other people's business for no good reason were stock characters in Latin comic literature. The writer Apuleius wrote a delightful tale, *The Golden Ass*, recounting the adventures of a hapless young man so curious about the divine mysteries of Isis that he accidentally gets himself turned into a donkey for a time. Augustine took a characteristically darker view of things, calling curiosity an inbred and insatiable *lust of the eyes*, a sin. Leaving sin aside, it is certainly true that we can enter states of willful curiosity so intense that we forget what we were looking for in the first place. It is like being trapped in a self-driving car.

Cervantes painted a memorable portrait of someone in this state of mind in "The Man Who Was Recklessly Curious," a story one character tells in *Don Quixote*. The tale concerns a wealthy Florentine merchant named Anselmo and his beautiful, adored wife, Camila, who loved him in return. Anselmo was a happy man, not least because he also had an old friend, Lothario, whom he trusted with his life. Yet after some years in his happy marriage, for seemingly no reason at all, Anselmo became plagued by the thought that his wife might not be as virtuous as she seemed to be and might betray him if given the chance. He could point to nothing, it was just a feeling, one he could not shake, that intensified with each passing day. And so Anselmo decided to put her devotion to the test and settle the matter once and for all. His idea was to persuade Lothario to try seducing Camila and then observe how she would react. After much arguing and resistance, Lothario reluctantly agreed and one day set to work, with Anselmo listening in another room. Camila passed the test and proved herself to be true.

But the conviction that his wife's apparent loyalty was just a ruse hiding something darker had gotten the better of Anselmo, and he couldn't leave matters there. He kept bringing Camila and Lothario together and even made Lothario write love letters to see if she would respond in kind. She didn't. Finally Anselmo decided to leave town in order to test her again, pressuring Lothario to make daily visits to Camila and report back to him. By then the couple really was falling in love, and the predictable happened: they ran off together, and Anselmo returned to find he had lost both a loving wife and a loyal friend.

Anselmo could offer no reason for distrusting Camila's heart. But usually we do our best to contrive reasons for refusing to obey a DO NOT ENTER sign. That is particularly true when we become conscious of the fact that another person put the sign there, someone with authority who has not thought it fit to consult us. Rather than consider the possible wisdom of the injunction and take it as an opportunity to pause and reflect, all we can see and feel at that moment is a challenge to our autonomy. Adolescents live in this state for as long as their sentence lasts, erupting whenever parents and teachers draw a line, however benevolently. We must pass through this trial twice, once as children and then again as parents of children. And as we know, some adults never grow up. Today they can be heard raging against even mild forms of censorship imposed by government and tech firms to keep harmful material off the internet, as if any regulation is a ticket to the gulag.

Still, we all have moments like this, when the veil before us seems no longer just a veil, a warning, but an assault on our personal dignity. Just as there is no argument without an arguer, so there is no veil without a veiler. We feel disempowered and compelled to let the world know that we exist, that we count, and that we won't be done to. In these moments, our will to knowledge undergoes a subtle change. No longer aimed at some practical end or inspired by wonder, no longer about the *knowing*, it is now entirely about the *willing*, the right to assert ourselves. So quickly can this emotion surge up that at times we can even find ourselves yanking at veils we ourselves have put in place. How often do we turn off our email and social media accounts in order to accomplish some task, and then, annoyed by this temporary limit on our freedom, open them anyway after a few minutes and feel a rush of liberation? It is as if we woke up that morning, looked ourselves in the mirror, and thought, *Who are you to tell me what to do?*

Apart from fear, probably the most unruly forces in the human psyche are pride and shame, which is why humiliation sets off such violent passions. But while we might live for long periods free from physical danger, psychological threats to our dignity are potentially in every human encounter. And every divine one, if the myth of Prometheus is to be believed. There are many versions of this ancient tale about unruly curiosity, but they all paint the portrait of two angry gods in a struggle for recognition and command. After Zeus offended Prometheus by failing to recognize his role in winning the war against the Titans, Prometheus got his revenge by bringing to human beings the fire that Zeus had denied them, out of fear that they might challenge his authority if they were able to see, to know, and to build. Prometheus also sent along a care package containing all the important arts and sciences: astronomy, mathematics, writing, animal husbandry—even prophecy and dream interpretation. And for this attack on his authority, Zeus famously chained him to a pillar, where an eagle would visit him daily and eat out his liver, which then regenerated itself overnight.

In some readings of the myth, Prometheus got his rightful comeuppance, and we will too if out of hubris we challenge the gods. In other readings he is a tragic figure, even a martyr, whose love for humankind brought our first enlightenment and secured our dignity. Whichever way we read the story, it is also a lesson about the power of shame and anger in motivating the will to know—and the will to keep people from knowing. Prometheus was driven by spite, not benevolence, after his pride was wounded. His curiosity was born of petulance. By bestowing enlightenment, he was arming allies, not multiplying loaves and fishes.

Prometheus's self-righteousness is characteristic of the hardened veil snatcher. Once someone's instinctive animus against limits to knowledge is transformed into reasons, however flimsy or transparent, that person can start to feel licensed to spread the good news and liberate others from the cave. Henrik Ibsen's play *The Wild Duck* is about this sort of messiah complex. The story revolves around Gregers Werle, a Norwegian businessman's son who has just returned home after an absence of some years. His reason for leaving was that he had discovered what for him were unbearable dark secrets about his family, the darkest being that his father sired a child by a maid and palmed off both mother and child to one of Gregers's unsuspecting friends. In the son's absence this little family seems to have flourished. True, they are poor, despite being surreptitiously, if stingily, supported by the industrialist. But they love one another, and there is no apparent reason why anyone should be the wiser.

Gregers, though, suffers what Ibsen calls *an acute attack of integrity*, the Norwegian national disease. Knowing the truth about the family's situation is unbearable to him, and all he can think to do is transfer his anxiety to someone else, in this case to his friend, to whom he reveals everything. To mask his motivations, he presents himself as a savior who, by puncturing the lies everyone has been living, is *laying the foundations of a true marriage.* Instead he destroys it. After learning the truth about the situation, his old friend leaves his wife and rejects the daughter he now knows is not his. The distraught child ends up killing herself. Gregers, though, is chillingly indifferent. When a character tells him, *Rob the average man of his life-illusion, and you rob him of his happiness at the same stroke*, Gregers can only reply, *If you are right and I am wrong, then life is not worth living.* Rather than pluck out his eyes, this self-righteous Promethean comforts himself with the thought that he is simply too good for this world.

THE WHIRLWIND

Trust in the Lord with all thine heart, and lean
not unto thine own understanding.

—Proverbs 3:5

The beginning of wisdom is this: Get wisdom.

—Proverbs 4:7

Playing hide-and-seek with ourselves can become a
perilous game, depending on what is being sought or
avoided. Oedipus's existential situation is a literal
matter of life and death. Battered by his will to know
his true condition and by his equally strong will to
evade that knowledge, he is utterly alone. There is no
hope of outside assistance, no court of appeal, and
no prospect of escaping himself. A mute Fate, which
stands even above the gods, has set the rules of the
game he is trapped in. The gods are absent, and he is
left to punish himself.

The tragedy of the young man who challenged Isis
is different. His passion for knowledge puts him in an
antagonistic relationship with an outside force, not an
inner one. It is the goddess's resistance to his wishes
that provokes his willfulness and causes him to make a

mistake fatal to his future happiness. A sad end, but a much less disturbing one. The dramatic roles are familiar and legible to us: the goddess Isis represents The Great Withholder, the one who knows and will not reveal, and the young man is The Supplicant who struggles against an unjust authority—an authority he also needs, since he is incapable of saying no to himself. He suffers from a kind of dissociation that is fortunate in the short run, sparing him Oedipus's self-torture, but unfortunate in the long run because his projection prevents him from internalizing the *No!* voice and making it his own. This is one classic theory of the birth of religion: we create parental gods as protectors but also as authorities to resist, thus postponing the hard work of becoming our own authorities.

This is the deepest psychological source of religious taboos against curiosity that societies have laid down since time immemorial. Given how fraught our inner struggles with the will to know can be, one can see how embedding those dramas in a grander theological story of our relations with the divine might come as relief. There is some comfort to be had in thinking that I am not alone in feeling self-divided, that division has been inscribed into the cosmos itself, setting Zeus against Prometheus, the One True God against Satan, the Children of Light against the Children of Darkness—it's all of a piece. This thought also gives me a fixed role to play in relation to the veil makers in the sky, as a free individual who must choose whether or not to obey an external authority. The psychological load of our not-at-oneness is thereby lessened. This is why we are taboo-creating, taboo-fearing, taboo-observing, taboo-breaking creatures all at once, though never at the same time. One hand of the psyche must never know what the other one is doing.

Consider the Garden of Eden story in the second and third chapters of the Book of Genesis. It is so familiar that it is easy to overlook the strangest, most basic thing about it: that the very same writer who conceived of the Tree of Knowledge of Good and Evil also conceived of the taboo against plucking its fruit. Why both? The Tree myth seems to be unique in world religions. We are familiar with taboos forbidding us to seek or do something in particular, but this one forbids us from acquiring a tool—knowledge— that we might employ for all sorts of purposes. One can imagine a god who withholds the most important knowledge from us, in which case striving for it would be pointless and we would be entirely dependent on him. Or one can imagine a god who cheerfully welcomes all inquiries and roots for us as we try to understand creation, ourselves, and him—in which case taboos would be unnecessary. But a god who dangles the possibility of knowledge before us, only to punish us for grasping at it? That sounds more like a human being. (If *God created man in his own image*, it must cut both ways.)

The entire drama of human curiosity, of wanting to know, fearing what we will discover, placing veils over discomfiting truths, and then ripping them off in an act of self-assertion is captured in just a few verses in Genesis. But, unlike Oedipus, we are given a chance to escape our inner curiosity dilemma by following a common script and obeying clear rules set by the creator of all things, who now bears full responsibility for setting boundaries and drawing veils before our eyes. Like all successful bureaucrats, we have learned to kick the hard problems upstairs.

> Might: Only Zeus is free.
> Hephaestus: I know. I have no answer to this.
> —Aeschylus, *Prometheus Bound*

The pagan gods loathe gawkers. One day the Greek hunter Actaeon was pursuing game in a wood when he accidentally happened upon the goddess Artemis bathing in a pool. Outraged by this violation of her nakedness, the goddess turned him into a deer, and he was mauled to death by his dogs. Then there was Pentheus, the king of Thebes, who took a dislike to the god Dionysus and officially banned his annual rites in the city. In revenge, the god induced madness in the king's mother and aunts, who then joined the Dionysians in the woods. Pentheus distrusted the cult's secret orgiastic rituals, but he was also curious about them, so he disguised himself and then climbed a tree to witness firsthand what was going on. He was almost immediately discovered by the women, who in their frenzy mistook him for a dangerous animal. Like Actaeon's dogs, they tore him limb from limb. His mother joined in.

The lesson of such stories is: *Know thy place.* But disrespect is not all that is resented by the gods we create; they also resent and fear our curiosity about the wider world and what we might learn to do. The Greek god of criticism, Momus, gives vent to both in an ancient Hermetic text called the *Kore Kosmou*:

> This species is curious of eye and loquacious of tongue; it will hear what is none of its business, will be greedy to sniff and destined to mishandle all that can be touched . . . Human beings will dig up the roots of plants and test the properties of their sap. They will investigate the nature of stones, dissect animals down the middle—not only unreasoning animals, but even themselves—in their desire to discover how they are formed. They will stretch out audacious hands as far as the sea, chopping down naturally growing forests to ferry themselves to the lands beyond. They will investigate what objects exist deep within temple shrines. They will hunt as far as heaven, wanting to observe the movement established there . . .

In the myths of the ancient Mediterranean and Near East, the tension between the wills to acquire and to avoid knowledge appears as a brute struggle for power in which the gods see us as competitors. These deities are not benevolent superior creatures, nor do they represent the best in us. If anything, they reflect us at our worst—petulant, vain, aggressive, jealous, capricious. They may occasionally aid a human being or develop an erotic attachment to one, but they do not love us, and we are not expected to love them. Beneath our polite relations, the burning of sacrifices, and all the rest is a contest for mastery in which knowledge proves to be a potent weapon. In such a world, seeking it is neither moral nor immoral, it is simply good strategy.

The Bible projects a different picture of the human situation. Here curiosity is also treated in what we today would consider moral terms, involving principles, reflection, intentional inner states, and the giving of reasons. The language of right and wrong, duty and dereliction begins to replace that of the contest of wills. The Hebrew God is portrayed as curious about the lives of human beings because he cares for them, not because he wants to exploit them. How curious we should be about him, in what ways and under what circumstances, is left frustratingly vague. An eleventh commandment certainly would have been helpful here, especially for theologians. For if curiosity is forbidden, we have no business seeking the *logos* of our *theos*.

At times the biblical God can indeed seem like just another Zeus, jealous of his power, and he certainly does enjoy a burning sacrifice. If he were not potentially in competition with human beings, he would not have become so apprehensive about them constructing the Tower of Babel. When God overhears the builders laying out plans to build both a city and the tower, hoping to make a name for themselves, he, like Momus, worries that this is just a start, and that soon nothing will be impossible to them. By confusing their languages so they could not succeed, God nailed a sign to the world: NO CLIMBING.

All things being equal, the biblical God also prefers to remain hidden from our curious, prying eyes. He leads the Hebrews out of Egypt in a pillar of cloud and speaks to them from within it, hiding his face; he delivers the commandments from another dark cloud; and he resides in the Holy of Holies of the Tabernacle, behind a curtain. Occasionally Moses is admitted into God's presence, but these encounters are rare and by invitation only. We read in the Book of Exodus that just before God delivered the Ten Commandments, he told Moses, *You have found favor in my sight.* Moses seems to have taken this remark as an invitation to a face-to-face visual encounter, and he responded by asking to see God in all his glory. The request was only half granted: God would show himself to Moses, but only while moving away. *You shall see my back; but my face shall not be seen.* The Bible may lack comedy and tragedy, but not irony.

* * *

In the end, though, the Hebrews' God is not just another Zeus. The divine-human encounter imagined in the Bible is largely discursive and dialogical, not competitive. God speaks, he reasons, and on at least one occasion—in a discussion with Abraham about the fate of Sodom and Gomorrah—he changes his mind. This is a deity who makes covenants with humans, which bind him as well. Though we are on earth and he is in heaven, there is constant rational and emotional intercourse between us, something approaching codependency. For once, the term *relationship* is apt, and like all relationships, this one requires interaction, movement, even work.

The Greek myths teach a prudential fear of unpredictable gods; sacrifices to them are little more than protection money owed to gangsters. The Bible teaches something radically different, a moral fear of the Lord—that is, a fear that in disobeying a just and loving God, we have done something absolutely wrong, and not just crossed a powerful, arbitrary figure. To fear in the biblical context means giving God the respect, awe, and obedience that such a God deserves, and doing so out of love for him.

> What has Jehovah your God asked of you, except to fear Jehovah your God, to walk in all His ways, and to love Him . . . Serve the Lord with fear and rejoice with trembling . . . The

> Lord takes pleasure in those who fear Him . . .
> I have loved you with an everlasting love;
> I have drawn you with loving kindness . . .
> You, Lord, are a compassionate and gracious
> God, slow to anger, abounding in love and
> faithfulness . . .

There is something sublime and morally beautiful about the reciprocal love between God and man as imagined in the Bible. But there is also something troubling about it, something bordering on passive aggression in this command to obey out of love rather than out of fear or good sense. (We know what happens to the children of parents who play mixed-up psychological games with love and authority.) The pagan gods are not interested in our intimate thoughts and feelings, they only want their way. *Don't look at me! Don't seek my power!* they growl. And we know how to satisfy them: follow their orders. But how to satisfy a lover? How to be sure that what we say and do and think will please and not offend? To love is to expose oneself to guilt. And there is plenty of it to be found in the Bible and the moral traditions it has shaped.

Poor Job felt the full weight of this guilt for having offended God, which only added to his material sufferings. At the beginning of his story, God, who loves Job deeply and is proud of him, makes a bet on him, allowing Satan to rob the pious man of his goods, his family, and eventually his health, all to demonstrate that he will remain faithful to the Lord. At first Job holds up remarkably well, even when his wife tells him to curse God. He starts to slip only when he falls into a testy conversation with some so-called friends who would like to debate whether or not God is being just to him. They are curious about the Lord's motivations, and by discussing them, they assume that these motivations can be fathomed. But who are these mortals to presume to judge God, even positively? Their conversation eventually provokes God to appear in a whirlwind and challenge their presumption. *Where were you when I laid the foundation of the earth? Tell me, if you have understanding.* Job is immediately humbled: *I have uttered what I did not understand, things too wonderful for me, which I did not know.*

How much this sounds like lovers' quarrels we've all had, with an outburst of pique followed by self-abnegation. Job repents in dust and ashes, ashamed of himself and his curiosity. The book ends with a snapshot of him posing with his restored lands and new children, a forced smile on his face.

> Do not rush to recite before the revelation is fully complete but say, "Lord, increase my knowledge!"
>
> —Quran 20:114

As projections of human double-mindedness about curiosity, many biblical stories can appear as moral and psychological advances over ancient pagan myths. If the tension we feel within ourselves is portrayed as a mere struggle for power between us and brutish withholding deities, it is difficult to learn to see ourselves in both sets of characters, as both wanting and not wanting to know. By imagining a loving God more like ourselves and reinterpreting the ground for taboos from divine fiat to intelligible moral care, we create an opening for eventually seeing that part of the art of living is knowing how to balance our dueling wills.

Yet this moral advance carries with it an important complication. If we love and respect the biblical God, there are certain things we will choose not to inquire about, such as what he looks like from the front, or why, of all things, he made a bet with the devil. As a general rule, we will trust the Lord and lean not on our own understanding. But almost immediately we will find that impossible. For loving God also means working to fulfill his commandments, which are intentionally general, in need of interpretation, and must be adapted to particular cases. If the Ten Commandments came with user directions and helpful diagrams, like mail-order furniture does, we would only have to follow the manual to do our duty. The Decalogue has none. And so we must use our minds and gain knowledge about the world to do God's will, which was probably his intent. And that opens new vistas for our curiosity. We had thought to kick upstairs the responsibility for limiting our desire to know, but as happens so often in bureaucracies, the memo was returned with instructions to work things out ourselves.

Let us assume only the absolute minimum: that we must seek God's face and explore his creation only in order to fulfill his commandments. In other words, curiosity is justified if, and only if, it is required for obedience. That seems a very narrow invitation to inquiry. But it is not. Consider just one commandment: *Honor thy father and thy mother.* What would we need to know in order to obey that divine injunction? A great deal, it turns out. We would, for a start, need to know what counts as honor, whether universally, in our particular society, or to the person receiving it. We would also need to know whether honoring fathers is different from honoring mothers. If honoring our parents includes looking after their physical well-being, we would then have to inquire into what constitutes health and what threatens it. For example, if a parent is suffering from dementia, we would need to learn what the condition is, how it progresses, and what treatments if any can mitigate the suffering.

To learn all that, though, we would need to live in a world where scientists and doctors make it their business to study such matters. For those specialists to acquire the basic scientific knowledge necessary to do their jobs, we would also need to live in a world where pure science is pursued by physicists, chemists, and biologists who consider it a good and noble thing to expose the wondrous workings of God's creation. And for those scientists to understand what counts as knowledge, and its limits, we would need people—call them philosophers—who occupy themselves with such abstract matters. Honoring our fathers and our mothers, then, would seem to require building a culture of curiosity.

The Bible at times recognizes curiosity as a condition of obedience, and a daisy chain of passages can be put together to emphasize just this. The prophet Hosea portrays God lamenting that the Hebrews had substituted the thoughtless making of sacrifices for genuine love of him and obedience to his commandments, which require reflection. The Book of Proverbs stresses the need for knowledge, particularly of wise dealing, righteousness, justice, and prudence. It even condemns whatever in us resists listening to the voice of wisdom:

> Wisdom cries aloud in the street; in the markets she raises her voice; on the top of the walls she cries out; at the entrance of the city gates she speaks: "How long, O simple ones, will you love being simple? How long will scoffers delight in their scoffing and fools hate knowledge?"

But it cannot be said that the Bible as a whole encourages a culture of curiosity, despite the fact that a great deal of knowledge is required to fulfill even the simplest of God's commandments. The reason is more psychological than theological. While the Bible preaches moral fear of the Lord, it does not address the experience of moral fearfulness. Even if fear is inspired by rational respect and genuine love, the habit of fearing can become a basic psychological disposition, and a paralyzing one. A person who thinks mainly in terms of obedience and transgression, and worries about betraying love, will not be inclined to ask too many questions, judging it better to keep eyes down and hope that all will be well. Sacrifice another lamb, perform the ablutions, be aware of what you eat, recite the prayers at the right hour, and that will suffice. The more fearful even a faultless believer becomes, the more he will be inclined to think of God as just another Zeus—a force to be appeased, not a Thou to my I.

The Bible can do a very good job of undermining itself. It often elevates our relations with the divine from an amoral power struggle to an interaction involving reason, respect, and feeling. But it can also spawn a culture of guilt-ridden, anxious fearfulness in which curiosity becomes morally risky. God's love can feel toxic in a way that the Olympian gods' indifference does not. With them, you always know where you stand (though keep an eye on your wallet). With him, you can feel watched, exposed, unsteady, trapped. Emancipation from a domineering, insinuating God can then seem an existential imperative, no less urgent than emancipation from a domineering, insinuating parent. When that happens, the urge to know, to be enlightened about what is, which might supplement and refine our faith in God, becomes confused with the urge for freedom, the impulse to assert ourselves against authority. We feel ourselves regressing to an early stage of our psychological development, back to the defiance of Prometheus, and our search for knowledge degenerates into a blind act of self-assertion—a way of standing before the divine whirlwind, shoulders back and legs apart, roaring: *Anch'io sono pittore!*

THE DEVIL'S BRIDE

There is then in philosophy, though stolen as
the fire by Prometheus, a slender spark, capable
of being fanned into flame, a trace of wisdom
and an impulse from God.

—Clement of Alexandria

But the devil's bride, reason, the lovely whore
comes in and wants to be wise . . . I trample
reason and its wisdom under foot and say, "You
cursed whore, shut up!"

—Martin Luther

Yet what if taboos restricting our curiosity are expressions of divine love, not arbitrary power? What if God's reluctance to show his face to Moses arose out of his benevolence? The young man who traveled to Saïs was initially possessed by a genuine, if undisciplined, passion for one, final Grand Truth, not a blind urge to transgress or to acquire Isis's power. His mistake was to infer from the veil and the goddess's curse that she was a capricious adversary who scorned him, and it was this perceived challenge that provoked him to overstep. That Isis might be his benefactor, that by veiling her face she might be trying to protect him from unknowingly harming himself, that the goddess might understand the human dilemma better than he does—this never occurs to him.

And it rarely occurs to us. That is not only because we are all built like that young man, with a BREAK IN CASE OF EMERGENCY alarm we can pull when challenged. It is also because we have inherited rival modern historical narratives that again reduce the taboo problem to a contest between authority and freedom. We in the West live in the shadow of a millennia-long conflict over the nature and legitimacy of curiosity that gave rise to new forms of philosophical and scientific inquiry whose fruits continue to benefit and disturb us. But even more, we live in a world bereft of concepts—and even language—for considering dispassionately the advantages and disadvantages of curiosity and taboos for life.

These master narratives that have come down to us were codified in Europe in the late eighteenth and nineteenth centuries, at a time when Prometheus was, quite literally, on everyone's mind. Marx wrote that he was *the most eminent saint and martyr in the philosophical calendar* and Nietzsche called him *man's greatest friend*. Goethe and Byron composed important poems extolling his daring, Percy Bysshe Shelley wrote a play, and Beethoven did the score for a ballet titled *The Creatures of Prometheus*. Mary Shelley was just joining the crowd when she added to the title of her dystopian *Frankenstein* the subtitle of *The Modern Prometheus*.

So it should not surprise us that a Promethean historical narrative about the progressive triumph of human curiosity developed out of this fascination. It combined Enlightenment optimism about reason and Romantic passion for defiant, free development. It cast as the Children of Light the freethinkers and scientists who over the centuries had resisted dogmatic authority and risked their lives to bring the fire of reason to human beings kept ignorant and incurious by the authoritarian Children of Darkness in sacerdotal garb. Thanks to their sacrifices, magic and superstition loosened their hold on the human mind, and modern medicine brought health to the human body. The mystical aura surrounding traditional authority dimmed, and people learned to mock irrational taboos that had once caused them to fear and tremble—and no dogma, however well defended by arguments and attested by miracles, can survive human laughter.* But the struggle for human autonomy is not over, the story concludes, and never will be. There is always some curious Galileo somewhere in need of defense, if not against religious dogmas then against tyrannical political ones. That is why there are no furloughs for the Children of Light.

---

* To amuse guests at his country house, Charles Dickens had placed in the library a number of empty books with fanciful titles embossed on them. Among the sets was *The Wisdom of Our Ancestors* in seven volumes: (1) *Ignorance*, (2) *Superstition*, (3) *The Block*, (4) *The Stake*, (5) *The Rack*, (6) *Dirt*, (7) *Disease*. Next to these he had placed an extremely thin volume titled *The Virtues of Our Ancestors*.

* * *

This account of the liberation of the human mind, based on all too true events and developments, was canonized in and for the nineteenth century. And like other powerful stories, this one generated a counter-myth that took Zeus's side. It rested on the same assumption as its adversary's: that when it comes to curiosity, there is a zero-sum struggle between autonomy and authority. Throughout the century, Catholic popes delivered *ex cathedra* encyclicals denouncing Promethean modernists who challenged Church teachings on nature and politics, and from the solitude of the Vatican promulgated extensive syllabi of errors. *Depravity exults; science is impudent; liberty, dissolute*, thundered Pope Gregory XVI in the 1830s.

But as science and democracy kept advancing, ever fewer Europeans were frightened by these lightning bolts. Far more effective was the contention that rather than empowering human beings, Prometheanism only dehumanized them. The avowed aspiration of the early Renaissance to insert human beings into the harmony of the cosmos eventually resulted instead in the disenchantment of the world, transforming God's benevolent order into a centerless whir of matter and forces obeying nothing but themselves. And human beings, taking their cue from this new cosmos, decided to obey only themselves and took pleasure in violating old taboos that had limited their pride and constrained their selfishness. That the celebrated

French Enlightenment was followed by the Revolution and the Terror should have surprised no one. The gifts of Prometheus have always been poisoned.

This humanistic critique of secular humanism had wider appeal, especially among bucolic Romantics convinced that immoderate curiosity about nature had only prepared the way for modern industrialism and vast, inhuman cities connected by smoke-belching trains that scarred the landscape and frightened the livestock. The socialists among them wanted to defend fundamental human dignity and social solidarity against the science- and technology-driven energies of capitalism, which dispossessed workers and gave rulers new powers to wage war and expand empires. This left-wing critique of modern science and the Enlightenment has more recently inspired a "deep ecology" indictment of the humanist tradition as a whole and points vaguely toward a posthumanist future, whatever that might mean. All demonstrating that secular anti-Prometheanism can be as fanatical and indifferent to the human good as its adversary.

Given the real prospect of environmental collapse owing to global warming, not to mention advances in genetic engineering that are giving us frightening power to remake our own nature, one would think that this would be a good time to reflect dispassionately on the consequences of our wills to know and not to know. Freed from worries about overweening gods, we are now in a position to consider the problem of curiosity as a genuine human predicament requiring a recognition of our own inner complexity and needs. Yet the historical tales of Prometheus bound and unbound still hold us in their grip, and we are subjected to futile jousting between futurists who deny the costs of freedom and apocalyptic prophets of Gaia demanding that we cede our place to mollusks. We seem stuck in an infantile repetition involving authority and self-assertion, unable to take full responsibility for ourselves.

Hope is a good breakfast, but a bad supper.
—Francis Bacon

The most significant veil in our lives has no human artisan. It is drawn between us and the future by time itself: we know that we will die, we don't know when. We also don't know how our lives would change if we had foreknowledge of that moment. If offered that knowledge, should we accept it? Should we rip off even this veil too?

The Nobel Prize–winning author Elias Canetti once dramatized this question in a short play called *The Numbered*. It is set in a community where, at birth, every child is given a secret name corresponding to the number of years he or she will live (Nine, Seventy . . .) and a closed locket said to contain the precise day written on a piece of paper. When someone dies, a high priest called the Keeper opens the locket, reads the date to himself, and declares it to be a timely death; if the person is not dead at the end of his predicted term, the Keeper comes and takes him away.

The play reveals how much our psychological and social lives are shaped by ignorance of how and when we will die. Remove that ignorance, and everything would be affected. The society in the play is stratified according to longevity, those with the higher numbers being the most sought after as partners. People also adapt their plans according to their known life spans, as do parents of children. The children destined to die young are left without education or supervision, while those destined to long lives are encouraged to take risks. There is no reason to murder anyone in this society, since the day of the victim's death has already been set and can't be changed. Deaths go unmourned; depression is rare. Certainty is the mother of serenity.

The play's action centers on a man named Fifty who decides to defy the Keeper, refusing to go quietly into the night when his appointed time arrives. The Keeper allows him one more day of life, so long as he affirms the Holy Law. But Fifty keeps on living. He also begins forcibly opening other people's lockets, to reveal that they are empty. He gains followers, who call him the Deliverer, and eventually the old Law is overthrown and everyone is taught that their life spans are undetermined. Knowledge has freed them from this illusion. And in a very short time, the social order collapses. People become anxious and unhappy; murder becomes a potentially rational act; the loss of loved ones becomes unbearable. Fifty realizes too late what he has done and asks the Keeper if there is any way to reverse the damage and restore the veil of the Law. There isn't. Knowledge, once it has escaped the box, cannot be put back in. Neither can fear.

Canetti's play, first performed in 1956, is an intriguing mind experiment about the value of veils. And the degree to which modern medicine has placed us in the position of the fictional people in this fictional land is striking. Today, individuals with potentially fatal illnesses can know, if they wish to, their odds of survival. The parallel is not exact, as our odds depend on what sort of treatments we choose to pursue. We have landed in the worst of both worlds, knowing more about our possible futures yet burdened with the weight of trying to actualize one of them.

Examples abound. Suppose you come from a family that has a high risk of developing an incurable hereditary disorder that manifests itself late in life, causes extraordinary pain and mental deterioration, and is always fatal. A genetic test has been developed that shows whether someone has the gene. Do you take the test? If you do, you will know with one hundred percent certainty whether you have the gene. If the test shows that you don't have it, you never have to worry about the disorder, nor will your children. If the test shows that you do have it, you must live with that knowledge and make decisions in light of it, including whether to have children. The other option is to restrain your curiosity and not take the test at all. Then you must live with absolute uncertainty—which might be preferable if you are good at putting things out of mind, but not if you are a brooder. Which do you choose: Knowledge or ignorance?*

* James Watson, the codiscoverer of DNA, knew where he stood on such matters. When he had his genome sequenced in 2007, he made sure that the value of his APOE4 genotype,

We are not well equipped to think about these problems. One reason is our heavy reliance on the language of rights and freedom to confront questions earlier societies saw in terms of fate and taboos. Should oncologists have a legal obligation to tell patients if they will soon die of cancer? Do families have a paternalistic duty to keep medical information from an ill relative if receiving it would shorten the patient's life? Do we have a right to what is called genetic ignorance if we might be prone to diseases like that described above, or are we obliged to undergo tests that might dissuade us from having children who might contract it? Listening to these arguments, one realizes that, given the inevitability of death, the contemporary moral discourse of choice and rights is inadequate to the task. Talk of Fate as a force in the world may be superstitious, but it does at least keep our eyes focused on the hardest truth.

We no longer have blind bards who sing tales of Fate from which we can draw wisdom for coping with these things. Today we only have people wearing lab coats. About four decades ago, behavioral psychologists began to study the benefits of positive illusions in the treatment of illness. At first, and in tune with the times, the consensus seemed to be that *staying positive* was crucial to patients' well-being; it improved intel-

which indicates the risk of developing Alzheimer's disease, would not be published. He also stipulated that it not be revealed to him.

lectual functioning, kept people motivated, made them more caring, enhanced their self-esteem, and even changed their views of the past. Of course, not all illusions have this effect. If I am unable to walk a tightrope between high buildings or swim across the Mississippi, I better not have any illusions about the matter. (As the researcher who used this example soberly remarked, for nonswimmers, *drowning is clearly maladaptive*.) But in most instances, when dealing with illness, there is a case to be made for selectively holding our inquisitiveness hostage. And some research shows that for certain illnesses, rates of longevity and survival are improved if doctors give a more optimistic diagnosis than might be warranted statistically.

More recently, though, researchers have focused on the possible harms of positive illusions. To begin with, not everyone responds positively to positivity. People who are inclined to a dark view of life and usually expect the worst actually appear to make better medical decisions once told bad news. Their depressive realism, as psychologists call it, proves a good preparation for dying, if not for living. For other patients, the problems lie elsewhere. Those who are given overly optimistic diagnoses in the early stages of their illness are less likely to seek out knowledge about it, and more likely to engage in risky behavior that might hasten death. Cancer patients with unrealistic expectations about their chances are also much more likely, as the illness worsens, to choose expensive and often toxic aggressive treatments that prove pointless. They are also less inclined to enter hospice care early enough to help prepare themselves and their families for death and to plan for those who will outlive them. Far too many of us die in intensive care, alone and in pain, attached to machines whose beeping is our only companion. Patients who receive palliative care do not live longer than those who refuse it, but the quality of their lives as they draw to a close is much better. Figuring out how to honor our fathers and mothers in such situations has never been harder.

One can only pity doctors who must deal with all this. Nothing in their medical training prepares them to practice the benevolent art of veiling that the gods once practiced for us. When fatal illnesses or genetic conditions were incurable or impossible to detect early, physicians bore no responsibility for deciding whether to order tests and inform patients of the results. There were also paternalistic taboos, as there still are in certain cultures, against needlessly bringing bad medical news. A survey of American doctors in 1961 found that an astonishing ninety percent did not feel obliged to tell their patients that they had cancer. What, from their point of view, would have been the point, given its incurability at that time? With the recent revolutions in medical knowledge and technology has come a revolution of rising expectations. Patients now expect their physicians to anticipate which tests should be administered in order to detect illnesses, even before symptoms appear. And if they do fall ill, they take it for granted (if they are adequately insured) that any and all treatments available will be administered to cure them. Most of these patients do not understand the intricacies of clinical trials and their often ambiguous results, or the nature of hypothesis formation and testing in science, or even basic probability. Which means they have no way of interpreting the results of any studies they happen to read about, or of judging hollow claims being made on the internet. Perversely, if improvements in therapeutics do not keep pace with improvements in testing and mortality prediction, then people will be saddled with an increasing stock of terrifying knowledge difficult to bear.

One can understand why, then, doctors who write about their experiences today say they are more hesitant to make clear, comprehensible prognoses than in the past, especially if those are negative. There are always more data to consult, more tests to be administered, more treatments to be tried or clinical trials to join, even if it means simply postponing the inevitable. We are all reluctant to hurt someone's feelings, and we all want to protect our own. An optimistic prognosis serves both objectives, at least temporarily. Even those trained in the sciences are understandably apt to fall into a kind of magical thinking or believe in self-fulfilling prophecies if the alternative is a difficult conversation or a feeling of failure. The more power our doctors have to predict and to cure, and thus the smaller role Fate seems to play in our lives, the harder it is for them to confront the remaining limits of their knowledge and power. The veils that once maintained their confidence are gone, too.

Perhaps it was this prospect and others like it that the young man in Saïs perceived after he ripped off the veil of Isis. Perhaps he saw that other veils would be undone by human beings just like himself, until none or very few would remain. That we would be left alone to master our wills to know and not know—without divine guidance or restraint. And perhaps that prospect caused him to dream that he was back in the temple, frantically trying to reattach the goddess's veil with tape, twine, or anything on hand. And that on the following morning, and every morning after that, he found the veil once more on the temple floor and Isis staring at him silently with her immobile, unavoidable eyes.

3

The Hollow Men

ON EMPTINESS

Truth, Sir, is a cow which will yield such people
no more milk, and so they are gone to milk the
bull.

—Samuel Johnson

Oedipus is in a hurry, and who can blame him? His
angry subjects are suffering from the plague, and he
has no idea why. There is no time to study the matter
in greater depth to discern if there is an organic explanation for the disaster, or whether it will pass in due
time. He is a king, not a professor who traffics in
hypotheses. A king must appear decisive, offer explanations, and comfort or placate those he cannot help.
When decisions must be made, we all become impatient with doubts, with *yes, buts*. When *yes* or *no* are
the words we need to hear, any other answer seems an
affront. Getting to *maybe* is the greatest cognitive
achievement human beings are capable of. But there
are times when it is too much to bear.

We are not made for living in uncertainty. Learning that *she loves me* is welcome news; learning that
she loves me not is unwelcome but at least definitive.
Learning that *she maybe loves me*—especially if combined with *and I'll never know for sure*—is, on the
other hand, an invitation to madness. That is what
gripped poor Anselmo in *Don Quixote*, who ruined
his marriage in a vain search for certainty about his

beloved. Perhaps he would have been better off consulting a wise, benevolent fortune teller who in seeing his distress would have assured him that Camila was the most devoted of wives and had no other lovers. That would have been kind. There are times when a voice from the beyond—that of an oracle, a prophet, a psychotherapist—is the only force capable of breaking the circle of doubt.

A confrontation with uncertainty is a confrontation with the limits of our knowledge, which the wisest of philosophers have assured us is an excellent thing. *It is of great use to the sailor to know the length of his line*, said John Locke, and he was right. So why are we so often foolish sailors? Why do we set off on the rough seas of empty speculation only to smash our reason against the rocks of the absurd? Because we are proud, certainly. It feels humiliating to admit that what we thought we knew, and have built our lives upon, and persuaded others to believe, is false. In Plato's dialogues, Socrates time and again tries to persuade those whose views he has refuted, or cast into doubt, that by learning the extent of their ignorance, they actually know *more* than they thought they did. He, too, is right. And still we resist.

The will to ignorance feeds off of pride and our fear of toxic truths. But it can also, paradoxically, feed off of our desperation to find the One Great Truth that will make all future inquiries unnecessary. It was overeagerness for secret final knowledge that got the young man in Apuleius's *The Golden Ass* turned into a donkey, and that ruined the life of another in Schiller's poem about the temple of Isis. When we find ourselves in a frantic state of wanting knowledge and have run up against what seem to be its limits, we become highly susceptible to any suggestion that there is a third way. It is then that our will to ignorance perks up and begins to purr: *All is not lost, you have been lied to. Of course you cannot reach certainty about the matters most important to you, if you imagine yourself armed only with reason and experience. But you are not. There is an "alternative" source of knowledge that will give you what you need. All you must do is find the secret path.*

> Now we have eaten of the tree of knowledge.
> But paradise is locked and bolted, and the
> cherubim stands behind us. We have to go on
> and make the journey round the world to see
> if it's perhaps open somewhere at the back.

For the German poet Heinrich von Kleist, this was a messianic hope. For the mystic, it is a conviction.

Though there are countless forms of mysticism, they share a common dramaturgy. The narrative recounts how our souls were once united with truth— call it God, the One, the Absolute—but at a certain point, lost in archaic time, these souls somehow became detached and fell into bodies and limited minds, which now stand in the way of our return to wholeness. The soul cannot hope to escape this condition by working within those limits by gathering experience, developing theories, and reasoning about them. It must instead undergo a difficult process of inner transformation. The soul has to be purged of all it thinks it knows and then be detached from the body, a terrifying experience leaving a profound sense of emptiness. But once it has passed through this dark night, the soul, now an empty vessel, is prepared to receive divine truth, either in a sudden epiphany or by undergoing a slow, progressive spiritual ascent leading to a reunion with the One. Some mystics use metaphors of moving from darkness into light, achieving divine illumination, or from sleep into true wakefulness. What they share is the conviction that their minds were once polluted by falsehoods and ultimately by the faculty of reason itself. And that now, having emptied themselves and silenced reason, they are in possession of esoteric knowledge unavailable to the rest of us.

The will to ignorance is a wily character and is not above masquerading as a more elevated will to knowledge. It makes the promise that if we abandon what little sure knowledge we possess, and silence the skeptical voice of reason within, we will be filled with a knowledge beyond all reason and experience. It preaches that emptiness induces insight, that hollowness is holiness. It feeds a fantasy of achieving a second innocence, where the tragic shadows of doubt and sense of limitations that fall over every adult life begin to clear and the sun shines directly on us once again without filter or mediation. Even if we are not mystically inclined, there are moments when we can become desperate to know and impatient with our inner limits. And then we find ourselves dreaming of a world where all we have to do is empty our inner houses, leave the back door open, and paradise will find us.

THE BAGPIPE AND THE SAGE

> It is a foolish custom, by which a man enabled
> to speak wisely from the principles of nature,
> and his own meditation, loves rather to be
> thought to speak by inspiration, like a
> bagpipe.
>
> —Thomas Hobbes

Asklepios, the Greek god of medicine, was notoriously difficult to reach. This posed an obvious problem for his devotees, who needed help the moment they got sick. And so, at the roughly four hundred temples devoted to his worship around the Greek world, a ritual called incubation was practiced to entice him into paying a house call. After undergoing a ceremony of purification, patients would be shown to beds in the holy sanctuary and then be left to sleep, emptying their minds completely. (Freud shakes his head.) The hope was that by seeing the sufferer worshipping him in this sacred place, Asklepios would appear in a dream and touch the stricken body, healing it. Or at least he would offer a diagnosis and prescribe a cure. When patients awoke, priests on the temple staff would devise therapies, based on the reported dreams, to be carried out in the town, which subsequently grew wealthy from the business. If the patient got well, it meant the dream had been sent by the god; if not, it meant the patient had to keep returning until a genuine dream came. Those who were cured were expected to write down their dreams and then pay a fee; any delay in payment would bring about a relapse. (How little medicine has changed.)

Dreams come unbidden; that is what gives them occult force. But it also limits their usefulness. People facing present dangers want to hear an authoritative voice they can draw assurance from; they want to be told what to do, and that all will be well if they follow directions. They also, understandably, want the gods to come when bidden and to be on time, which the gods have just as understandably resented. Speaking out of the whirlwind, God in the Book of Job makes it clear that he is not a vending machine. He shows his face and reveals his plans when the time is ripe and to whom he chooses, not when we demand it. We must learn to *wait upon the Lord*, the Bible tells us: patience is piety. But the history of religion— and not just of religion—is the history of human impatience.

The will to know *now* has been a fertile mother of spiritual invention. It inspired many societies to look to the natural world to discern things unknown, developing methods for deciphering signs and training individuals to interpret them consistently. For millennia, specialists were taught to do this by taking auspices from the disposition of stars in the sky, from decks of cards, dice, a pile of sticks, a candle flame, a bowl of oily water, or the entrails of some unfortunate animal. In such places divination was taken to be a teachable skill, and becoming a professional did not require any inner transformation or unusual inspiration. In the classical art collections of our museums one sometimes runs across astonishing and amusing pedagogical tools that were developed for seers in training. They include large models of animal livers cast in metal, with helpful lines demarcating areas where abnormalities indicate divine meanings. With these devices in hand, no one needed to wait to hear from the gods. Discerning the future was a self-service activity.

Mute signs properly interpreted can tip the balance of people's reasoning, but there is something much more powerful and reassuring about hearing direct divine speech. Unlike seers with their tool kits, or freelance soothsayers in the marketplace and mediums who communicated with the dead, oracles were thought to have a talent for emptying their minds so completely that they entered a state of divine madness (*mania*) in which the god spoke directly through them to others. The most highly revered oracle in the ancient world was the Pythia at the Temple of Apollo at Delphi, which is why Oedipus consulted her. Legend has it that the Pythias were originally young virgins chosen because their ritual purity and innocence could be assumed. But after a petitioner fell in love with one Pythia and raped her, it was thought safer to transfer the office to elderly women made to dress up as virgins. When it came time to respond to a petitioner who had placed a precise question before her, the Pythia would enter the inner sanctum of Apollo's shrine and seat herself on a tripod erected over a crevice in the ground, out of which inebriating gases were said to rise. (Another tradition has her chewing on hallucinatory plant leaves.) These fumes paralyzed her rational faculties and put her in a trance of receptivity that allowed Apollo to speak through her in cryptic remarks and riddles. Oracles in other places reached this state by different means, such as the virgins of Larissa, who would periodically let themselves be possessed by Apollo after drinking the blood of a young lamb.

Sacred rites and age-old traditions ensured that not just anyone could set herself up as Apollo's mouthpiece. Any society that believes gods can speak through human beings faces the challenge of vetting oracles and keeping their utterances within acceptable bounds. At Delphi this was accomplished by placing an intermediary between the petitioner and the ecstatic to ensure that the latter's pronouncements did not inspire extravagances. This *prophetes* was tasked with listening to the Pythia's enthusiastic speech, translating it into ordinary verse, and, one imagines, censoring it as needed. It was an ingenious way of preserving the occult power of oracles while bringing their messages more into accord with reason and convention. Press secretaries perform the same function for gaffe-prone politicians today.

Oracles are both a blessing and a curse to the peoples who consult them. They promise direct access to truth by skirting the limits to human understanding, whether through intuition or mystical insight or ecstasy. Yet if the society is not to be rent by noxious, conflicting revelations, oracles must be somehow approved and bounds to interpretation set. Call it the Vatic Imperative. We face the same imperative today with the psychologists and psychiatrists who help us interpret our dreams. They can be reimbursed by insurance companies only if they are trained and licensed by the state and if their diagnoses can be made to fall within categories established by the *Diagnostic and Statistical Manual of Mental Disorders*. (All the problems of modern bureaucracy are foreshadowed in the history of archaic religions.)

One way to satisfy the Vatic Imperative is to fuse political and prophetic authority. A ruler can declare himself to be a prophet, or a prophet can seize power or found a new state. A modern example was Mao Zedong, whose Little Red Book became revealed scripture for fanatics of the Chinese Cultural Revolution, with terrifying consequences. Ancient examples are the Abrahamic faiths, whose prophets—Moses, Jesus, Muhammad—also founded kingdoms (though

Jesus's was not of this world). This arrangement has great political advantages while the prophet-kings are alive, but it poses a challenge when they die, taking their theological-political charisma with them. *Have the gods fallen silent?* people start to wonder. Is a new revelation in the offing, annulling the first? Or must the society now be ruled within the bounds of an established body of revealed truths that can perhaps be augmented but never contradicted or annulled?

The great medieval theologians and philosophers of Islam and Judaism gave much thought to this question, which is not of mere antiquarian interest. Their debates revolved largely around the nature of the prophet himself and the role of reason in his activity. One school held to what might be called the Empty Vessel theory of prophecy. Its view was that God chooses as his true prophets those who—owing to their piety, modesty, and faith—put up no resistance to the divine message and add nothing merely human of their own to it. We can trust the Empty Vessel perfectly because he trusts God perfectly. For some, the primacy of emptiness even meant that otherwise positive human attributes like intelligence and experience could pollute the message. There is a Muslim tradition that Muhammad was actually illiterate, which is why, the story goes, God chose him to transcribe the Quran, since he was incapable of changing a word. Mormon missionaries are apparently taught something similar. They are encouraged to tell potential converts that Joseph Smith's lack of schooling is proof of the veracity of his intricate revelation, which a simple nineteenth-century farm boy in Upstate New York could not possibly have contrived on his own. (Which seems to underestimate both the imagination of boys and the uncanniness of Upstate New York.)

The second school of thought worried about the first school of thought. It was concerned about the potential political and spiritual dangers that irrational rogue enthusiasts posed and the bad example they might set. If the faithful got it into their heads that, by emptying themselves of reason and law, they too could experience God without mediation, they were liable to become susceptible to their own idiosyncratic ravings and contaminate others with them. And so this school developed a Great Man theory of prophecy, which held that God reveals things only to the most wise. These rare individuals then use their gifts to interpret the divine messages rationally (like the *prophetes* in Delphi), then translate them into terms that ordinary believers can comprehend. The assumption was that since at some point reason must enter the transmission of revelation, only intelligence and good judgment, not emptiness, are signs of the true prophet. The Jewish sage Maimonides offered the most elaborate defense of this Great Man theory in his twelfth-century *Guide of the Perplexed*, where he set the bar for authentic prophecy very high—so high that only Moses fully satisfied its conditions. Yes, there were later prophets who were used by God to call Israel to repentance. But Moses was something more: a statesman and quasi-philosopher.

In the end, the Great Man theory of prophecy triumphed over the Empty Vessel theory in the orthodox Jewish and Muslim traditions. Moses and Muhammad are revered today as the wisest of men, not the hollowest, and mystical movements such as Hassidism and Sufism are still viewed with some suspicion. Orthodoxy holds that revelation is the end and not the beginning of our innocence; it is the beginning and not the end of our task of thinking. But the Empty Vessel theory survived at the fringes of these orthodox traditions, for reasons that are also understandable. If the prophet is the quintessentially rational person, chosen for that reason to deliver God's rational dictates, one begins to wonder why we need God at all. Why not just a profound philosopher or a team of researchers? Nothing necessarily needs to be revealed to us by an outside force, we just need very, very smart people to work very, very hard to find the truth.

But a link to online research papers is not what people seeking divine authority and assurance want. They are desperate to hear a voice from beyond that intervenes in the here and now, reveals what cannot be seen or understood, and promises mastery over it. Which is why a prophecy that runs against the grain of reason, delivered by someone who has abandoned his rational faculties, might strangely seem the more

authentic voice of God. In those moments, the bagpipe has a clear advantage over the sage.

> You will not recognize the writing while you
> are doing it as it is the writing of the spirit/
> entity that you are allowing to communicate
> through you . . . Those of you who choose to do
> your automatic writing on the computer have an
> advantage as you will be able to save the work
> you do on a disc. Make sure you get in the habit
> of printing out your writings once they are
> written. Spirit has been known to erase writings.
> Why this happens no one knows.
>
> —Irene Richardson

> Where now is Greece, with her big pretentions?
> Where the name of Athens? Where the ravings
> of the philosophers? He of Galilee, he of
> Bethsaida, he, the uncouth rustic, has overcome
> them all.
>
> —Saint John Chrysostom

Christianity never produced a Moses, and for a very good reason: Jesus was the incarnate Word of God. After his mission was completed, the early Christians believed they had no further need of official prophets, pagan or Hebrew. Their relations with God, no longer mediated by law, were democratized and individualized, and their intercourse with him was conducted in private or within small communities under the guidance of the Holy Spirit. And since they expected the Messiah to return soon, they were not inclined to reflect on the political implications of the new arrangement. The age-old problem of vetting oracles and designating prophets could be thought to have disappeared overnight.

Quite the contrary proved true. The Messiah's return was delayed, and then delayed again. And as direct memory of his mission faded and the Christian faith spread and confronted challenges all religious communities face, the need to hear authoritative divine speech became pressing once again. But something had changed. Now, rather than there being one voice designated to channel God's advice and commands, any and every believer could plausibly claim to be God's Empty Vessel. And over the centuries, untold numbers have. It would have taken a Christian Maimonides to sort this all out and bring the prophetic impulse under the guidance of reason and political responsibility. Instead, God in his wisdom sent to the young Church Paul of Tarsus, who heaped scorn on the learned and idealized the blessed emptiness of those he praised as fools. His writings became the petri dish in which a distinctive strain of anti-intellectualism developed within Christendom and thrives in our secular age. It is no exaggeration to say that the history of Western populism—spiritual and political—began with Paul.

Nor is it an exaggeration to focus on one particular passage from his First Letter to the Corinthians as the source of all the mischief.

> For Christ sent me not to baptize, but to preach the gospel: not with wisdom of words, lest the cross of Christ should be made of none effect . . . For it is written, I will destroy the wisdom of the wise, and will bring to nothing the understanding of the prudent. Where is the

wise? Where is the scribe? Where is the dis-
puter of this world? Has not God made foolish
the wisdom of this world? For after that in the
wisdom of God the world by wisdom knew
not God, it pleased God by the foolishness of
preaching to save them that believe . . . Let no
man deceive himself. If any man among you
seems to be wise in this world, let him become
a fool, that he may be wise. For the wisdom of
this world is foolishness with God.

One imagines Paul sitting at his table having just written these sentences, pleased by their rhetorical complexity and clever juxtapositions. And one can
imagine the Christians of Corinth unrolling his scroll
and feeling both satisfied and stupefied by his perfor-
mance. They certainly would have understood what
he was getting at. At that time Christianity was being
scorned and mocked by articulate, highly educated
Roman elites who were skeptical of a marginal sect
that attracted fishermen, tentmakers, publicans, and
slaves. The teachings of Jesus presupposed nothing
about a person's intelligence or level of culture. He
held up as spiritual models innocent children, uneducated workmen, and lambs with vacant eyes, forever enshrining reverse snobbery as a Christian virtue.
Paul in his letter seemed to want to buck up the side
against pagan contempt and make the early Christians confident in the new teaching. Any fool who
believes can be saved: this was the Good News.

* * *

The holy fool is a stock figure in many religious and folk traditions, and examples abound in Judaism and Islam as well. Many of the Christian fools one can read about (it is a large literature) were clearly suffering from some kind of mental illness, and it is sobering to see how readily believers over the centuries have projected sanctity onto them. (Today the fashion in medical circles is to diagnose them retrospectively as autistic.) This was particularly true in the Russian Orthodox Church. The *iurodivye*, as they were called, first became prominent in the eleventh century, and over the next five hundred years more than thirty of them were officially canonized as saints of the Church. Foreign visitors to Russia would record with astonishment the sight of these figures, who could be seen running naked around cities and towns in midwinter, unwashed and unshorn, dragging enormous chains and babbling incoherent sentences that local believers took to be prophetic. Their outrageous behavior was no less imaginative than their names: Johann the Hairy and Merciful, Isaac the Cave Dweller, Johann Big Cap, Vasilii the Barefoot, and Nicholas of the Cabbages, who was known for throwing vegetables at other holy fools encroaching on his territory.

One undeniably charming fool in the Catholic tradition was Brother Juniper. Juniper appears in *The Little Flowers of Saint Francis*, a medieval collection of legends about the life of the saint and his early followers that is still read today. The life of devout poverty is given epic treatment in the tales about Francis, the wealthy and educated bourgeois who tossed it all over to serve the poor, heal the sick, and preach to the birds. The comic anecdotes about Juniper extol a different moral ideal—intellectual poverty. We read about him playing seesaw with children while the townspeople mock and laugh at him; now he is giving away precious gold altar decorations to the poor, while the priests fume; later he is found cooking two weeks of food to save time for prayer, not realizing that the food will spoil. In perhaps the most famous story, Juniper cuts the feet off a live hog to cook and give to a sick friar who asked for pig's knuckles for dinner. The hog's owner, discovering his dead, trotterless animal, was understandably livid, and he complained. Saint Francis saw the man's point and tried to explain to Juniper why such an act, while well-meaning, was wrong. To no effect. Instead, the naïve friar went to the owner and asked him to surrender the rest of the hog, so that one act of charity might be followed by another. And the owner, now ashamed of himself, did just that, butchering the animal and donating it to the friars for the injury he had done them by getting angry. All Francis could say was, *Would to God that I had a forest of such Junipers*.

But in Paul's highly influential passage on foolishness in the First Letter to the Corinthians, he was less concerned with giving moral saints like Juniper their due than in puncturing the pretensions of the learned.

Paul represented a new human type in the ancient world after the advent of Christianity, and a recognizable one in our own: the cultured despiser of culture. Though well-read in Greek philosophy and trained in the Jewish law—he had been a Pharisee—Paul pretended that none of it mattered. Caught up in his own rhetoric and weakness for paradox, he seemed to be calling the already learned and cultured to scorn their gifts and adopt a willful ignorance instead, checking their critical faculties at the church door. A learned fanatic of the highest order, Paul made possible the transformation of the Gospels' beautiful moral ideal into an anti-intellectual ideology that was enshrined in the Christian scriptures and has since passed into our secular societies. That ideology has attracted a certain sort of mind ever since—one with a death wish.

> I have been crucified with Christ; it is no longer
> I who live, but Christ who lives in me.
>
> —Galatians 2:20

Paul's apologists over the centuries have tried to downplay his radical rhetoric and suggest that the contrast between the simple fool and the cultured mind was meant simply to teach the latter some humility, something we all should learn. But Paul aimed to do much more than that. He not only believed that the learned resist God; he believed that by emptying themselves of human knowledge, Christians could create an inner vacuum that would draw in esoteric knowledge bestowed by the Holy Spirit. Behind his thinking was a pneumatic or hydraulic conception of the soul, common in many mystical traditions, that sees it as a kind of storage tank with a fixed capacity, which must be emptied of its pollutions before it can be filled with the truth. As Saint John Chrysostom, a fourth-century devotee of Paul, put it, *We must restrain the inopportune raving of our own reasoning, make our mind empty and devoid of secular learning, so that we can offer it cleansed and ready to admit the Divine words.*

The oldest mystical traditions were elitist by nature; the spiritual labor required to pass through the dark night of the soul and be reunited with the One is great and must draw on uncommon inner strength, determination, and training. This is why mystics so often spoke of themselves as an elect, as the ancient gnostics did. Christianity, though, has a democratic conception of the religious life and presumes the equality of all believers in the eyes of God: any fool can be saved. Brother Juniper was a living symbol of the simplicity of the faith and the workings of God's benevolent *agape*. But the Franciscans never treated him as a font of wisdom: we are meant to learn and be improved by watching him in action, not by parsing his utterances for meaning. Paul's spiritual innovation was to fuse, through an alchemical process all his own, the notion of the blessed ignorance of the many (Juniperism) with that of the divine knowledge of the few (gnosticism) and make of it a seemingly coherent doctrine of the Christian life. Emptiness is next to godliness, fine. But now we learn it is also next to esoteric divine knowledge.

This is how Paul put it in his First Letter to the Corinthians:

> Yet among the mature we do impart wisdom, although it is not a wisdom of this age or of the rulers of this age, who are doomed to pass away. But we impart a secret and hidden wisdom of God . . . And we impart this in words not taught by human wisdom but taught by the Spirit, interpreting spiritual truths to those who possess the Spirit . . . The spiritual man judges all things, but is himself to be judged by no one. *For who has known the mind of the Lord so as to instruct him?* But we have the mind of Christ.

When the Hebrew Bible speaks of the "Spirit of God," it is just a metaphor of how God in his oneness exercises his power for those who love and fear him. There is never any suggestion that this spirit inhabits human souls, a pagan notion of the sort Moses was determined to stamp out. But the early Christians, as we see in the legend of Pentecost, did believe that God's spirit could descend and inhabit their own. Paul endorsed this view, and it allowed him to perform what can, not inaccurately, be called a theological bait and switch. In the opening chapter of the First Letter to the Corinthians he warned the faithful against the temptations of proud Greek wisdom and called them to a life of intellectual humility and even foolishness. In the next chapter, though, he dangled before them the prospect of a privately experienced divine knowledge, unassailable by reason or the judgment of others. Again, *The spiritual man judges all things, but is himself to be judged by no one.* The implications of this second passage proved just as revolutionary as the first. It made plausible, and certainly very attractive, the prospect that after emptying themselves of human wisdom and experiencing an infilling of the Holy Spirit, the Christian faithful would be transformed into God's esoterically enlightened deputies, with a license to descend on the world like a posse of whirlwinds, bringing God's truth and judgment down on benighted sinners everywhere. *It is no longer I who live, but Christ who lives in me*: Was there ever a more dangerous theological potion concocted for spiritual tyrants?

A play on words is a dangerous thing. It can reshape a life, even an entire civilization, if it is memorable enough. Which is why, ever since he wrote, Paul's most radical phrases have become slogans chiseled into the minds of Christians who cherry-pick his writings: *I will destroy the wisdom of the wise . . . If any man among you seems to be wise in this world, let him become a fool . . . We have the mind of Christ.* Damage control efforts within the Catholic Church eventually succeeded in counteracting some of the antinomian and anti-intellectual bile in Paul's writings. The legacy of these efforts were vast edifices of learning that still exist today: monastic libraries, universities, and schools for children.

But as the Reformation showed, it takes only a small dose of Paul to undo the work of centuries. Among the ironies of that spiritual revolution is that the gale winds of Pauline inspiration unleashed then have never stopped blowing through Protestant churches. Whenever a Protestant denomination begins to settle in, establishing authoritative institutions and centers of learning and adding complexity to its theological doctrines, there almost inevitably arise within its ranks little Luthers who denounce *the devil's bride* and set up their own denominations, allegedly modeled on the primitive Church with its inspired simple souls. Which is why the history of Protestant denominations, running down to the ecstatic Pentecostal movements of our time, resembles nothing so much as a children's game of leapfrog, where the point is to keep one step ahead of the truant officer who would send them back to school.

And Paul's slogans continue to shape the secular-democratic thinking of many today. One hears echoes of them in the populist conviction that it is the aggressive philistine, and not just the simpleton, who is the possessor of esoteric insight. One sees it at work in the fallacy, precious to anti-science fanatics, that the more ignorant a believer's opinions and ideas might appear in the eyes of the educated world, the more likely they are to be correct and of divine origin. And one only has to list some of Paul's theological principles to recognize their affinity with the degraded politics of our time: the equality of all believers, justification by faith, blessed ignorance, the pointlessness of learning, the sanctity of inspiration, secret wisdom, the unassailability of inner conviction. The bagpipes now hold the floor, and the sages have fallen into embarrassed silence. One can only hope that Brother Juniper is somewhere praying for us.

> This little light of mine, I'm gonna let it shine.
> This little light of mine, I'm gonna let it shine.
> This little light of mine, I'm gonna let it shine.
> Let it shine, let it shine, let it shine.
> —Traditional American gospel song

LEGION

In the back of the large auditorium were a number of hippies. One of them got up and started towards the front . . . Turning to a stranger sitting next to me I whispered, "Is that man in the spirit of the Lord?" He replied, "I don't know, but he surely doesn't look too good." "Why, he has a demon!" I exclaimed . . .

As it happened the long-haired hippie came to the platform, took over the microphone, and lifting his hands in the air declared, "I am the Way; I am Jesus." Then everyone knew he had a demon.

—F. & I. M. Hammond, *Pigs in the Parlor:*
A Practical Guide to Deliverance

The more strongly one believes that the soul is permeable and can be filled by the Holy Spirit, the more likely one is to believe, as a fifteenth-century physician once put it, that devils *go in and out of our bodies, as bees do in a hive.* This was as true in Jesus's age as it is in our own. The Gospels tell us that one of the first things Jesus did after being baptized was to cast out an unclean spirit possessing a man in a synagogue, to the astonishment of other Jews attending. Later, when people were threatened by a mad tomb dweller who'd been infected by spirits that gave him superhuman strength, Jesus approached the man. His demons cried out, *What have you to do with me, Jesus, Son of the Most High God? I adjure you by God, do not torment me.* Jesus asked their name—*Legion, for we are many*—then granted their request to be sent into a herd of two thousand pigs, which ran toward a cliff and ended up drowning in the sea.

Obsessions with demons tend to appear in moments of historical or religious crisis, setting off panics and then fading away. The modern Enlightenment and the scientific revolution took their toll on these superstitions, and by the nineteenth century demon panics became rarer in Europe and even in the United States, where the experience of the Salem witch trials had gained a prominent place in national memory. But just before the turn of the twentieth century, something strange started happening. Though Western countries were rapidly secularizing, the idea of the permeable soul or mind, subject to outside forces, not only survived but flourished. Fascination with the unseen spirit world returned, and a great, unexpected wave of occult spiritualism swept through. Ouija boards sold out, séances were common, and mediums made good money conjuring up departed spirits on demand. And those who could not afford a medium could consult popular books explaining how to empty and fill oneself with spirits in the comfort of one's own home. The freelance spiritualism that began then is still with us. A national poll in 2012 revealed that well over half of all Americans now believe in the possibility of demonic possession.

This is no doubt related to the popularity of Pentecostal and other charismatic movements that grew up in Protestant and Catholic churches in the 1960s. These groups perform "baptisms in the Holy Spirit" and cultivate speaking in tongues and other ecstatic practices mentioned in the New Testament, including exorcism. Most of this is freelance work, though there are also well-known (and well-off) specialists who run "deliverance ministries" and publish popular guides for spotting those beset by demons and releasing them from bondage. There are even charismatic Christian psychotherapists who claim the "power of discernment" and make the binding and casting out of demons part of their therapeutic practice.

The Catholic Church hierarchy has been unable to ignore the new obsession with Satan among its faithful around the world. In the 1960s the Church stated its intention to revise its three-century-old exorcism ritual (the Rituale Romanum) in order to centralize the authorization of exorcisms and limit them to medically and psychologically trained exorcists. The aim was to further marginalize the practice. But work on the new ritual dragged on, and it was not promulgated until 1999, by which time such books and movies as *The Exorcist* were lending credence to beliefs in the omnipresence of the demonic, as well as in the shamanistic power of Catholic priests, who briefly became heroes.

To meet a new demand for exorcisms, the Church now finds itself having to train more people to cast demons out, and it works with the International Catholic Association of Exorcists, which accredits Catholic, Anglican, and Orthodox clergy, along with laypeople, as Exorcist, Religious Demonologist, and Paranormal Research Teams. In Italy alone, it has been estimated that half a million Italians consult exorcists every year. The exorcist for the Archdiocese of Indianapolis told a journalist in 2018 that he had received seventeen hundred phone or email requests for exorcisms in that year alone.

Which is madness. But a consistent madness. When Saint Paul idealized the fool who empties himself of worldly wisdom to be filled with the spirit, he did not let on that this might be a risky operation. Central to his legacy in our culture is the optimistic assumption that self-abandonment is safe, that what fills us after we leave behind what we know will necessarily be good. But if one accepts that every soul is a conduit for spiritual forces, if every man and woman—and, why not, every child—can be his own Isaiah, then the witch-hunters, the demonologists, the tongue speakers, and all those who quake at the mention of Satan and fear for their lives actually have it right. If the soul is open to spirit, it is open to any spirit. So beware. As Paul himself wrote, *even Satan disguises himself as an angel of light.*

> It is one of God's more ordinary leadings in the
> ways of grace to permit the devil to possess or
> obsess souls which He wishes to raise to a high
> degree of holiness.
>
> —Jean-Joseph Surin

Anneliese Michel was born in 1952 in a small Bavarian town in Germany. Her parents were extremely
conservative Catholics who belonged to fringe groups
that later rejected the reforms of the Second Vatican
Council. Because Anneliese came out of this milieu, it
was not surprising that after high school she began
studying to become a religion teacher.

But at the age of seventeen, already depressive, she
began to experience epileptic seizures that became
progressively worse over the next four years. They
were soon accompanied by visions and voices, in psy-
chotic episodes that neither psychiatric care nor drugs
could relieve. At this point an older family friend who
belonged to a Marian cult invited Anneliese on an organized trip to a pilgrimage site, unrecognized by the
Catholic Church, where the Virgin Mary was said to
make regular appearances. On this trip the family
friend became convinced that Annaliese was possessed,
and she planted the idea in the young girl's mind. After
that, friends thought her much changed. She became
more reclusive and much more devout, and she joined
a conservative prayer group. Her condition worsened:
her body would suddenly stiffen, she fell into trances,

she had visions of the Virgin. She and the family friend began meeting with a local priest, who had also become convinced of her possession, and he petitioned his superiors for permission to perform an exorcism. It was rejected. But the next year—about the time the film version of *The Exorcist* reached Germany— Anneliese began displaying what were conventionally thought to be "classic" symptoms of possession: unable to enter church, she avoided the crucifix, snapped rosaries, and knocked pictures of Jesus off the wall. In 1975 the bishop of Würzburg finally granted the priest permission to cast the demons out.

By this time Annaliese had begun sleeping on the floor and refusing to eat. Soon she reported seeing demons, and sometimes she crawled under tables, barking like a dog. She bit the head off of a bird and licked up her own urine. Over the next year the exorcism ritual was carried out secretly in the Michel home more than sixty times. During many of these rituals the attendant priests took photos of Anneliese and taped conversations with her demons, conversations that can now be found on the internet. The photos show a frightened, extremely emaciated girl in bed, with dark, self-inflicted bruises around her eyes. On the recording one hears a deep, ungodly voice roaring and screaming and the attempts of the exorcists to engage with the demons. Yet despite the repeated formulas, despite the showers of holy water, they refused to depart. Anneliese died on July 1, 1976, the feast day of Saint Simeon the Holy Fool. The coroner determined the cause of death to be malnutrition and dehydration. She weighed sixty-eight pounds.

The response of German authorities to Anneliese's death was swift, the scandal large. A trial was held, and in 1978 the priest as well as the parents were convicted of negligent homicide for failing to call in doctors. They were sentenced to six months in prison (later reduced to three years of probation). The German Bishops' Conference reviewed the case and declared that Anneliese had not been possessed, and in 1982 they promulgated new rules for dealing with those who believe they are.

Yet the drama continued. During Anneliese's parents' trial, a nun in another part of Bavaria reported having a vision of the girl's miraculously preserved body in her grave. Under the pretext of putting her corpse into a better casket, the parents had their daughter exhumed, only to discover that her body had significantly decomposed. After the trial, and shortly before his death, Anneliese's father built a chapel in memory of his daughter where masses using the pre–Vatican II liturgy are sometimes held for pilgrims who come from all over Europe by the busload to commemorate her and leave messages asking for her help. *Anneliese, you chosen flower of suffering, be my intercessor with God and pray for mercy for me.*

The idea that Anneliese was a martyr arose quickly after her death. One of her exorcists, a vocal opponent of the Second Vatican Council, declared, *She heroically took her suffering on for Germany, for the young (who lay close to her heart), and for priests who had abandoned their calling.* Anneliese's mother also believed this. She told an interviewer, *I know that we did the right thing because I saw the sign of Christ in her hands. She was bearing stigmata and that was a sign from God that we should exorcise the demons. She died to save other lost souls, to atone for their sins.*

To those devoted to her memory, Anneliese Michel was as holy as the saints who once kissed the sores of lepers, an innocent who became the vessel, not of the Holy Spirit, or Apollo, or Asklepios the healer, or the Greek muses, but of the demonic. When Jesus was told by a disciple not to let on that he was the Messiah, he resisted, saying, *Get thee behind me, Satan!* For reasons only God knows, Anneliese was chosen to let him in. When she died at the age of twenty-three, this Brother Juniper of the dark side fulfilled her calling.

BRUISED FRUIT

A poet is someone who manages, in a lifetime
of standing out in thunderstorms, to be struck
by lightning five or six times.

—Randall Jarrell

The reason people believe in inspiration is that they experience it all the time. Ideas come to us, after all, not the other way around. It's surprising how little we think about this. We routinely use such passive-voice phrases as *it occurred to me* or *it struck me*, without considering their inherent occult potential. Cartoonists have it right when they convey the experience of having a thought with the image of a light bulb going on by itself. Thinking is not a matter of planning to think *X* and then doing so; *X* suddenly appears in the mind, seemingly unbidden, inviting us to think it. Every moment of our conscious lives is a *Eureka!* moment.

So it should not surprise us when some people report that they hear voices; we all do. The trouble begins when they try to speak about this uncanny experience as if they understood why it happens and then invest their experience with authority. There is something both amusing and disheartening about how many mystics who undergo *an experience beyond words* then go on to write thick books explaining "that of which nothing may be said." (Something about uniting with the One seems to loosen the tongue.) Poets, too, face this temptation to speak about what speaks to them, though the prudent have always been circumspect, expressing themselves indirectly. In the very first line of *The Iliad*, Homer calls upon the divine muse to speak through him as he takes up the unenviable task of dealing with the anger of Achilles. That is the last we hear of their interactions. William Blake summed up his work method in two sentences spoken to a friend: *I write when commanded by the spirits and the moment I have written I see the words fly about the room in all directions. It is then published and the spirits can read*. End of story.

It's extraordinary, when one comes to think of it, that people have felt the need to gild the lily of artistic inspiration with the heavy lead of explanations. Once an aesthetic epiphany has taken place and found expression, what more really needs to be said? There is a touch of resentment in even the grandest encomium to the arts, as if the prosaic needed to assert its privileges against the poetic. Ever since the Renaissance, talk about artistic inspiration has threatened to drown out the voices of the inspired—or, worse, to transform them.

Plato is largely responsible for this: *The god takes the mind out of inspired poets and uses them as his servants, as he uses oracles and divine prophets, so that we hearers may know it is not they but the god himself who speaks*. While this passage was for centuries taken to mark an elevation of the poets to a quasi-divine status, in truth he was demoting them to civil service jobs as postal workers. To the prosaic soul, there is something threatening about those prone to streams of powerful inner experiences, sender unknown, which they struggle to capture in images that come *tapping at the window*, as André Breton once put it. The deepest among them have always resisted being domesticated by any theory, however flattering, of what it is exactly that happens to them. They feel bound by an ethics of the epiphanic.

The medieval sages of Judaism, Islam, and Christianity made it their business to work out such an ethics for divine prophecy. When modern artists try to articulate one for themselves, it is striking how much they sound like theologians and mystics, despite their efforts to resist the gravitational pull of religious language. What they seem to be after is a way of expressing awe and wonder without invoking an author of the awesome and wonderful or pointing to suspicious divine fingerprints. They experience the miraculous in a cosmos that they believe has no miracle maker, and they feel an inner obligation to maintain the integrity of that experience and not bruise its fruits. I wonder how many are aware that they are struggling with the same dilemma all mystics do when the numinous experience is over—that of finding a way to live in a world where the only trace left of the explosion is a crater in which nothing else will grow.

* * *

And then there was Hugo von Hofmannsthal. Known today mainly as the gifted librettist of Richard Strauss's operas, Hofmannsthal's poetic career began in his teens, when his learned and heavily symbolic verses were celebrated by the leading poets and critics of the late nineteenth century. But at the age of twenty-seven he underwent a crisis that robbed him of the desire and confidence to write poetry. And so he largely abandoned it, leaving behind as his explanation a fictional letter he published in an art magazine in 1902. No document I know of evokes more powerfully the burdens of inspiration.

The fictional writer is a young poet named Lord Chandos, and he is responding to a letter from his friend Francis Bacon. It is 1603 and Bacon has not heard from Chandos in several years, so he writes to express his concern, and to encourage his friend to seek medical help for whatever melancholy is preventing him from writing. Chandos replies that he feels separated from the author of his early works by a chasm and that the poems *dance before me like miserable mosquitos*. He is embarrassed by the groundless confidence and ambition he felt just two years earlier, when he conceived a grand literary project to be titled *Nosce te ipsum*—know thyself. Now he says, *What is man, that he conceives projects!*

What overtook Chandos in the intervening period might be described as a kind of poetic aphasia, leaving him progressively unable to use common words he had used confidently his whole life. Words like *spirit* and *soul*, even *good* and *bad*, suddenly seemed inadequate to describe anything at all. It was not that the world had become meaningless to him. Quite the contrary. It now appeared so overfull with significance that ordinary things—the skin on his fingertip, a watering can left out in the rain—had suddenly taken on a *sublime and moving aura* that left him speechless. He felt everywhere the presence of something unnameable that *fills any mundane object around me with a swelling tide of higher life as if it were a vessel*. Within himself there surged a vast empathy for this something.

It was not easy living this way. Yes, there were moments of *mysterious, wordless, infinite rapture* but also a kind of terror of frightening off the feeling of the marvelous, which left him hard, distant, empty. Revelation is a burden; no wonder so many prophets retreated into caves after having had their say. In marvels begin responsibilities, and now Chandos understood that his was to fall silent. He had received no esoteric knowledge to pass on, he served no god as postman, nor was he hosting any demons. He had learned to let his experiences happen, to leave them untouched, unsullied, unexplained. *Eureka!*

4

Lambs

ON INNOCENCE

Truly, I say to you, whoever does not receive
the kingdom of God like a child shall not
enter it.

—Mark 10:15

Innocence is like a dumb leper who has lost
his bell, wandering the world, meaning no
harm.

—Graham Greene, *The Quiet American*

Before setting out for Moriah, where he intends to
obey God's command and sacrifice his son, Abraham
loads the wood into Isaac's arms and carries the
burning torch and a sharp knife himself. On the way
his son asks, *But where is the lamb for a burnt offering?* The question is devasting, as is Abraham's answer: *My son, God will provide himself a lamb.* It is
a scene of unspeakable cruelty. (The murder of Abel
is a crime statistic by comparison.) For Isaac is doubly
innocent. Unaware of God's command, and presumably too inexperienced to beware of fathers bearing
torches, he is psychologically innocent. And since he
has presumably done no wrong, he is morally innocent as well. All this weighs on Abraham, and is meant
to. He has agreed to be the hand by which innocence
is extinguished.

There are other traditions in which a father might

kill a son without qualms, whether to gain divine favor or to ensure a military victory. But the Hebrew
Bible is a different sort of book. Its God is a test giver
who keeps an eye on the moral spectator. Isaac turns
out to be just a prop in a drama revolving entirely
around his father. Once Abraham has proved his infinite resignation before God—without, in the end,
committing the unspeakable—nothing more is required of the human lamb, and the incident is not
mentioned again. The veil is lifted from Isaac's eyes,
and he goes on to become an adult saddled with two
difficult sons of his own. One wonders if he ever
thought back to that strange afternoon. He certainly
would not have been encouraged to dwell on it. In
Judaism there is no cult of the innocent lamb.

In Christianity there is. The Gospels rewrite the
Abraham drama and present a divine Father who, for
mankind's sake, willingly sacrifices his divine-human
Son, who just as willingly offers himself up. In this
version, the Father is the prop, and the innocent Son
is the story. *Behold the Lamb of God, which taketh
away the sin of the world!* So declared John the Bap-
tist on first seeing Jesus, echoing the words of the
prophet Isaiah centuries earlier, who proclaimed that
the Messiah would be *brought as a lamb to the slaughter.* Jesus spoke of himself as a *good shepherd*, not as a
lamb. But John was working from a different script, one
in which the Messiah was destined to be beaten, lashed,
spat upon, and crucified. A self-immolating Isaac.

Good Shepherd imagery appears very early in Christian iconography, beginning with catacomb paintings showing the Redeemer with one lamb draped over his shoulders while two others accompany him. It implies that lambs are vulnerable and ignorant creatures in need of continuous protection and guidance. But by the later Roman Empire, the image of Jesus as the sacrificial Lamb of God became more common, and it ended up leaving an ambiguous mark on Christian consciousness. Anyone who has experienced injustice or loss can identify with the wounded Lamb of God, perhaps drawing solace from the thought that there will be a reckoning in heaven, thanks to his sacrifice. And some may even find a perverse satisfaction in reenacting his sufferings as a means of inner purification. But how can a wounded creature protect and guide the faithful? Where is the righteous anger Jesus displayed when driving the money changers from the Temple? The Yahweh of the Hebrew Bible is a fearsome God, leading his captive people out of the wilderness in a pillar of cloud to the lands they will conquer. Has that God absented himself, leaving Christians a lifeless animal as his sentry? Or does the Lamb of God have another side?

This question must have preoccupied some early Christians, for painters and sculptors soon began to portray the Lamb of God exercising supernatural powers, raising Lazarus from the dead, multiplying the loaves and fishes, baptizing other lambs, and even receiving the Ten Commandments on Mount Sinai. He had died, but he was not dead; he had been weak but now was strong. This tension between messianic sacrifice and messianic redemption—call it the Two Lambs Problem—is captured with stunning beauty in images of the *agnus dei*, showing a defiant animal standing on an altar, with a triumphal flag flying overhead—and its blood flowing into a sacred chalice from a wound near its heart.

Yet nothing in the Christian Gospels prepares us for the apocalyptic lamb in the mystical Book of Revelation, a repulsive exterminating beast with seven horns and seven eyes who has been sent to settle every divine score. After the creature opens the book of the Seven Seals, which reveals and brings about the end times, those slain for the Word of God emerge from darkness, demanding vengeance against their killers, which they will soon have. The rulers and the rich who oppressed them try to escape judgment and cry out, *Hide us from the face of him who is seated on the throne, and from the wrath of the Lamb!* No one answers, and they are doomed to eternal suffering. When the dust settles, the prophet looks out and the destruction has been swept away. He sees a new heaven and a new earth. The lamb is still there, though he has been cleaned up and is about to be given in celestial marriage to the New Jerusalem. *And the city has no need of sun or moon to shine upon it, for the glory of God is its light, and its lamp is the Lamb.* That, and its defense force.

> The modest Rose puts forth a thorn:
> The humble Sheep, a threatening horn.
>
> —William Blake

PEARS

Eternal wisdom goes where all her children dwell.
But why? How marvelous! A child she is as well.
            —Angelus Silesius

The scene in the Christmas crèche is so familiar that it takes some effort to realize how strange it is. The exhausted parents we recognize. But who are these silk-robed and turbaned men who bow and kneel before an infant? And what about the animals, who seem just as mesmerized as the visitors? Even the little lamb approaches and leans its head over the manger to get a look at the competition.

We are all Magi when it comes to children. Like other animals, we are hardwired to protect our young. But the subjective feelings that accompany this instinct point to something beyond mere preservation of the species. How we imagine children to be turns out to reflect how we imagine the world ought to be, which is what makes the death of an innocent child (or, for some, that of an unborn fetus) so hard to bear: a possible world, a better world, seems to have died with it. Even the death of other species' young disturbs some people. They will eat beef and mutton, but wouldn't think of touching veal or lamb. It is difficult to discern in what sense grown animals are less innocent and worthy of protection than young ones, given that the latter will face the same fate as the former if they reach maturity. One might even make a clever case that eating lamb or veal saves the animal from months or years of suffering in captivity.

But that's not what such feelings are ultimately about. They are about holding on to a world picture. The child in the cradle has no idea what a burden it already carries for us. We are inclined to saddle children with expectations that their new lives might somehow redeem our own, or redeem life itself. We are always on the lookout for occasions to rejuvenate our hopes in rejuvenation, from wedding days to Inauguration Days. They are all opportunities to convince ourselves that this time it really will be different.

We oscillate between two ways of thinking about the newborn before our eyes. One is to see it as a blank slate, knowing nothing, intuiting nothing, having neither moral nor immoral instincts (or only weak ones). This can fill us with a sense of promise as we project its life into the future—learning more, feeling more, discerning more. We can be hopeful about its prospects. But if we think of its innocence instead as the presence of something of infinite value, a kind of purity or moral perfection, then more melancholy thoughts will occupy us. Not because we see something dark in the infant's eyes, but because we imagine that its perfection can only be diminished or lost over time. If we assume, as one seventeenth-century English writer expressed it, that *the Child . . . is the best copy of Adam before he tasted of Eve or the apple*, it would seem to follow that *the older he grows, he is a stair lower from God.*

On this assumption, infants are not starting a journey into a world that they will make their own through experience and reflection on that experience. Rather, they stand as an alternative to our fallen world, a symbol of what we might have been had we not succumbed to it. Knowledge drawn from experience— perhaps especially knowledge of death—threatens to leave permanent stains on the sheets of their souls, as it has on ours. And so it must be postponed, blunted, diluted. *Save the children!* This might mean protecting them from harm until they can protect themselves, which is our obligation; or it might mean that we should preserve the childlike within them, or within ourselves, or within our society. That we should hold up innocence as a civilizational ideal and stave off knowledge of our intractable world.

> What children we still are, Kolya! And . . .
> and . . . how good it is that we're children.
> —Fyodor Dostoevsky, *The Idiot*

Ancient documents tell us that in the Mediterranean world of the first century BCE, adults used children as spiritual mediums in the theurgic ceremonies of mystical cults. A child would be selected for the job and blindfolded, and then the cult's adepts would begin secret incantations to entice the divine to make its presence manifest. This was one of them:

> Come to me, you who fly through the air, called
> in secret codes and unutterable names, at this
> lamp divination that I perform, and enter into
> the child's soul, so that it may receive the immortal form in mighty and incorruptible light.

This done, the blindfold would then be removed and the child would be asked to look into a flame or a bowl of oily liquid and report to the adults whatever he or she saw in it. The assumption was that children, lacking experience, were less likely to be blocked by their own thoughts and feelings and illusions, and thus were purer conduits for unadulterated truth. We make the same assumption whenever we say *out of the mouths of babes*, unconsciously quoting the Psalms. It is a very old thought.

So is the thought that children have special insight or divine powers. Consider the ancient legend of the Etruscan child-god Tages. The story goes that in the distant past, farmers in Central Italy were plowing a field a little too deeply when a god with the face of a child suddenly sprang out of the furrow. As people gathered around, the god began to speak and proved to be a sage. The elders copied down what he said, and that record became the guiding principles for Etruscan soothsaying ever after. A similar scene is recounted in the Gospel of Luke, when the young Jesus disappears for three days during a family trip to Jerusalem during Passover. His parents search for him frantically and finally find him in the Temple, arguing with the learned men there. His cool response when Mary scolds him is that he was simply about his Father's business. Not only is the child preternaturally wise, the adult is clueless.

It's extraordinary how deeply this assumption about children has marked our culture. Hollywood grows fat on it, producing movie after movie about visiting aliens and the children who have premonitions of their arrival. The creatures, who look like stretched-out infants with very large heads, instill no fear in them. Grown-ups in such movies are portrayed as oblivious or resistant, their age and experience having closed their minds. Except, of course, for the one exceptional adult who has never really grown up.

Another sort of adult—one in need of redemption—appears regularly in children's books such as *Heidi*, the nineteenth-century Swiss story that remains a perennial favorite and has spawned many imitators. In these stories, an innocent, preferably dimpled little girl is put into the care of a gruff old man. The adult treats her abysmally at first, but little by little he is transformed by the child's relentless, not to say tiresome, good cheer and good deeds. The cherub turns her cheek this way and that until the man begins to see how cruel he has been, but even more how he has darkened his own life. How? By refusing to look on the sunny side. The story ends with a tearful embrace between innocent child and the now healed adult.

And why not? If the Messiah came as a child, why shouldn't the psychotherapist?

> A seven-year-old child—he'd have cast the first stone.
>
> Michel Houellebecq, *Submission*

No parent of a two-year-old or a thirteen-year-old will be taken in by the myth that children are naturally good, honest, pacific, sympathetic, and wise. The market for it is expectant couples, forgetful grandparents, and the childless. But in truth, innocent goodness is not all we project onto children. We also burden them with our fears about evil in the world. One night we watch movies about wise toddlers giggling with aliens; the next, ones about demon-possessed infants and child killers. What we have trouble doing is holding in our heads a more complex view of the moral puzzle that all children are from birth.

The evil child, the one who murders his parents, who burns down the house or tortures the cat, haunts the imagination. He confronts us with everything we prefer not to think about ourselves and our supposed original innocence. The ancient world seems to have had less trouble recognizing children's capacity for wickedness. Even the Hebrew Bible contains a story about it. In the Second Book of Kings we read of Elisha, who has just taken on the mantle of prophet after Elijah had been taken up to heaven in a chariot of fire. One day, while making his way to the city of Bethel, Elisha runs into a large group of boys who tease him and mock his baldness. He does not turn the other cheek, though, nor does he use the episode as a teaching moment. Instead he curses the boys *in the name of the Lord*. Immediately two bears appear out of the forest and maul them to death.

The infant-besotted New Testament keeps children's capacity for cruelty at bay. Jesus suffers the children to come to him and exhorts his disciples to be like them. But the repressed always returns, and does so dramatically in the noncanonical Infancy Gospel of Thomas from the second century BCE. The author obviously wanted to extol the power of the muscular, avenging Lamb of God, but in doing so cast children in a darker light. The hero/antihero of this strange work is the preadolescent Jesus, who is portrayed with almost cinematic vividness as a bad boy. We first find him cursing a child found messing up something he had built on the sand; the boy shrivels up like a tree. When another boy inadvertently bumps into Jesus while running, he drops dead on the spot. Seeing what a menace the young Savior was turning out to be, parents of the other children in the village complain to Joseph and Mary, only to be struck blind. Finally Joseph stirs up his courage and confronts his son. *Why do you do such things?* he asks. The child only stares at him stonily and replies, *Do not vex me.* More than one parent will recognize this scene.

Perhaps in the early centuries of Christianity, when pagan realism was still a force, it was easier to confront the gap between the symbol of Jesus in the manger and the actual children adults have to cope with. Saint Augustine did so in his *Confessions*, presenting himself as a selfish, crying, petulant creature from the start. *So tiny a child, so great a sinner.* Of course, baby Augustine did not know what he was doing and could not tell right from wrong at the time, so was not morally responsible. But adult Augustine believed that the innate impulses he displayed at that age showed that willfulness, selfishness, and even cruelty are fundamental to our being. He told a now-famous story: One day he was playing with a group of friends, and they decided to steal some pears from an orchard. They weren't hungry and threw the pears away immediately. Why? *I had no motive for my wickedness except wickedness itself . . . I loved the self-destruction, I loved my fall, not the object for which I had fallen but my fall itself.* That was radically evil, and he was just a boy.

This assertion seems ludicrous to secular people today, who no longer accept notions of the fall or original sin. But the problem remains: How *are* we to explain evil in children? We try to block out the thought that a young boy can pull on a ski mask, load his gun, walk into a school cafeteria, and kill classmates he was joking with the day before. To explain this, we cannot point to the world created by evil adults as the culprit, since they, too, were once children; we face an infinite regress. The real difficulty is accounting for the fact that anyone is capable of evil *at all*. Augustine's deepest moral insight here—and it was the point of the pear story—was into the unprovoked gratuity of evil. We do some bad things in search of pleasures, like sensual enjoyment or social recognition, or out of fear. We do others in reaction to earlier traumas for which we are not responsible. Such acts can be terrible, but since they are explicable, if not defensible, we can't quite call them evil. Radical evil we commit *just because*: that is what makes it radical. And our capacity to commit it for no reason at all is innate. Blessed ignorance of the world will not prevent it from staining our souls. That is a very hard teaching but a necessary one, Augustine thought, if we want to understand ourselves. Yes, there are many joyfully innocent children in the world. But among those sitting at the feet of Jesus were surely a few who later preferred Barabbas. A serpent hides in the wool of every lamb.

> After an account of the heaven of good
> children, a small boy asked his mother whether
> she did not believe that, after he had been good
> a whole week in heaven, he might be allowed to
> go to hell on Saturday evening to play with the
> bad little boys there.
>
> —Ellen Key

PUTTI

> Prudery is the pretension to innocence without innocence.
>
> —Friedrich Schlegel

We are all inheritors of the Christian outlook, like it or not. We may not believe that Jesus was the Christ and that he sacrificed himself that we might have eternal life. We may not believe that sin is bred in the bone of all fallen creatures. We may not believe that we are spotless lambs, or vile serpents. Yet we are still entwined, psychologically and culturally, in the unhealthy dynamics of the Christian innocence ideal. Nowhere has this been more evident than in our thinking about the sexuality of children.

At times we find ourselves making the assumption that children are born naturally pure, the sheets of their souls unstained by desire. Parents and teachers then have one clear task: they must preserve children's sexual ignorance until they are adults. Most societies embrace some sort of censorship to delay sexual knowledge until the young are considered prepared to cope with it—or at least they used to do this, until the internet ripped away all benevolent veils. Christian societies—and now our post-Christian ones—practiced bowdlerization, allowing books to circulate so long as they were drained of content that might be construed, however indirectly, as corrupting. This defacement acquired its name from the work of Harriet Bowdler, a pious Englishwoman and editor of *The Family Shakespeare, in which nothing has been added to the original text; but those words and expressions are omitted which cannot with propriety be read aloud in a family* (1818). One of the earliest of expurgated books for children was a seventeenth-century French edition of the Roman dramatist Terence's plays, with the delightful title *Comedies of Terence Made Very Decent While Changing Very Little.*

If, on the other hand, we assume that the soul is assaulted from an early age by sinful sexual urges that constitute rebellion against the divine, censorship will be insufficient. Unruly sexual thoughts and practices would in that case have to be combated more explicitly, whether with shaming or punishment. This conviction was behind Christian campaigns against one sexual practice after another over many centuries. Masturbation is a good example. In the fifteenth century, Catholic educators were warning against it, especially in schools where boys had begun boarding together, although at the time it was considered at most a venial sin. By the beginning of the seventeenth century, and particularly among Puritans in Britain and the United States, masturbation became a Christian obsession that lasted well into the twentieth century. Pedagogical and child-raising manuals warned against the dangers of hysteria and the loss of bodily essence from masturbation, and circumcision was highly recommended. In some books, mothers were encouraged to bottle-feed their children, give them short baths, avoid long hugs, and even cut short conversations that might make boys in particular too attached to them. Outdoor activities were encouraged, too, though some writers worried that youth organizations might offer occasions for homosexual activity. In the nineteenth century, inventors developed grotesque gadgets that would keep young boys from touching themselves or having wet dreams while asleep. The obsession was so great, and so widely shared, that in 1894 it was thought reasonable in the State of Kansas that eleven boys in a mental institution be castrated simply to keep them from masturbating.

At the beginning of the twentieth century Freud tried to free us from this perverse dialectic. His insight was that in Western societies, double-mindedness about children—now idealizing them as pure and innocent, now treating them as depraved and inclined toward sin—was preventing the young from becoming autonomous adults with healthy sexual lives. He wanted to remove the moral valence from early erotic impulses, including those toward self-pleasure, and he portrayed them instead in the context of a lifelong process of sexual maturation that required the integration of drives and experiences. If childhood goes well, he reasoned, there is a good chance that the adult's sexual life will go well, too. Maturity, not liberation of the libido, was Freud's goal. Yet, as we know, this was not the message readers and even some of Freud's collaborators (such as Wilhelm Reich) chose to hear, and in the revolution of sexual mores that began a half century ago, free sexual exploration went from being considered an early stage in childhood development to being a life ideal for many adults—with the result that the pursuit of a second innocence for parents ended up robbing many children of their first.

The intrusion of images of sexualized children into popular culture of this period is a good example. Under the guise of open-mindedness, but in pursuit of titillation, Hollywood in the 1970s started making movies in which child actresses portrayed prostitutes, with shocking realism. Blatant sexualization of young girls in advertising became omnipresent, showing prepubescent girls in billboard and magazine ads wearing tight jeans, topless, with hands covering their half-developed breasts, blow-dried hair, and makeup, looking knowingly into the camera. *Nothing comes between me and my Calvins.* Far from Madison Avenue, in parts of America where one might have expected more resistance to these trends, beauty pageants started being organized in which girls under ten years of age were transformed into miniature seductresses, singing slightly risqué songs and making suggestive dance moves at competitions. Indecency was continuously defined down, as was parental responsibility. A former Miss Vermont Junior Queen, when challenged by a writer for putting her child in competitions, offered this memorable reply: *Do I put makeup on her? Yes. But I don't think I overdo it for a 5-year-old.*

Some of those taboos have been restored, thankfully, though in the language of individual consent rather than divine decree. It is no longer permissible, at least in the United States, to show sexually suggestive naked children in films or even in art photography. Pedophilia has become a national concern, and the lives of those convicted of it have been turned into prisons even after they have served their time. If anything, American parents now have exaggerated fears about the sexual dangers their lambs face outside the home. Yet—such is our double-mindedness about sexual knowledge—they are far less vigilant against threats within the home. Parents who drive their children to a nearby school *just in case*, and demand that they be allowed to bring phones to school *just in case*, also provide them with unblocked internet connections, giving them access to porn sites where young boys can see the sadistic sexual abuse of women, and teenage girls can post provocative images of themselves that any pedophile can see. Save the children, indeed.

O sweet and sacred Childhood, which brought
back man's true innocence, by which every age
may return to blessed childhood and be
conformed to you.

—Guerric of Igny

The Hebrew Bible forbade the public sacrifice of children and constrained the power of parents over their
sons and daughters. It proclaimed in no uncertain
terms that our children are not extensions of ourselves; they are dependent creatures who must be protected until they can live autonomously. Without this
moral advance it is hard to imagine modern child labor laws, obligatory schooling, and international
campaigns against child abuse, sending boys into battle, and killing children to harvest their organs (as
still happens). Yet that advance came with a corollary:
every license to innocence must one day expire. We
are meant to love our child, not become one.

While it obliges us to protect the young, Christian
teaching also invites us to think of them as symbols
that can orient us in a world no longer innocent. We
are encouraged to see them as visitors from a prelapsar-
ian past, ours and that of the species, and their ignorance as some sort of divine blessing. And when
children fail to follow the script of our fantasy, the
image flips, and they become bearers of the bad seed
planted in our souls. It is not hard to understand why
we have so much trouble getting childhood right. And
also, therefore, getting ourselves right.

Childhood is a powerful symbol, just as birth and death are. But actual children are not symbols of anything. They do not stand for the moral purity of the species or for its spiritual fallenness. They are not exemplars or fonts of wisdom, and they are not capable of healing our inner wounds. They are not *for us* at all. Yes, they are spontaneous, playful, graceful, and insouciant in ways we no longer can be and often wish we were. But innocence-talk is adult talk; it has little to do with what living and breathing children actually are. Children have no concept of childhood, any more than they have a notion of what they want to be when they grow up. (They make things up so we stop pestering them.) They are physically weaker, psychologically less developed, and unaware of the degree to which things are not always as they appear. And so we have the double task of keeping them from immediate harm while preparing them for independent adulthood.

Certain societies, present and past, have made the process easier by establishing public rites of passage to structure the journey from birth to death. Childhood in these traditions is treated as a discrete stage of development and is given its full due; then, at a certain arbitrarily fixed point, the child is forced to move on to the next discrete stage, whether to adolescence or directly to adulthood. Boys and girls usually undergo rituals at puberty to mark that moment, after which new things will be expected of them in society, new things will be due them, and certain behaviors will no longer be acceptable. They begin to acquire knowledge of the adult world they will need to navigate. In societies that structure their members' lives temporally in this way, children are not considered innocent lambs or fallen sinners; they are just on their way, like the rest of us.

No such script exists in Western societies today. Rites of passage are still practiced within the Catholic Church and Judaism, but participation in them is voluntary. Graduation rituals in our meritocratic societies are hollow pantomimes of those rites, and they do not set the rhythm of individual development in society at large, nor do they establish moral boundaries between stages of life. So it is not surprising that we are simultaneously confused about how to carry out our responsibilities to children and about what it means to be an adult. We seem to have settled instead on keeping everyone in the perpetual limbo of adolescence, rushing children into a state they are unprepared for, and allowing adults to remain there as long as they would like. Peter Pan would feel right at home.

WOLVES

The wolf also shall dwell with the lamb, and
the leopard shall lie down with the kid; and the
calf and the young lion and the fatling together;
and a little child shall lead them.

—Isaiah 11:6

For paradise to be possible either the lion
must lose his nails, or the lamb must grow his
own.

—Hans Blumenberg

Everyone needs experience with experience. The
ultra-pious who appoint themselves protectors of the
innocent labor under the illusion that life is a siege that
can be survived only by retreating behind high walls,
whether to the cloister, the Orthodox yeshiva, the
Wahhabi madrassa, the gated community, or the home
school. The illusion behind their illusion is the old psychology of mimesis, which holds that acquainting
people only with good things will make them good,
and banishing all bad things will keep them from
turning bad. Even Plato gives the impression of having believed some version of this. But it is false: the

more good one wants to do in the world, the more knowledge of evil one needs.

Historically, the greatest adult victims of these prophylactic illusions have been women, who have been secluded and kept ignorant of life in many cultures and on many and shifting grounds. In the early Christian era, convents were established by women to encourage spiritual contemplation and to serve others, which they did. But over the centuries they also became dumping grounds for poor families who were unable to afford dowries, or even food, or for rich families wanting to keep their daughters somewhere safe before marriage. With rare exceptions, young nuns received little formal education unless they managed to learn Latin (something few priests were willing to teach them), and no informal education on how to deal with men, property, politics, or much else in the outside world. And they certainly learned nothing about their own sexual desires, which could be satisfied only in illicit ways. By the eighteenth century, a large European literature had developed chronicling the misadventures of young girls sent to convents at an early age, where they either had a sexual awakening (proving the futility of seclusion), were sexually abused (proving its perversity), or remained ignorant, only to be preyed upon by unscrupulous men when they left.

Much has changed for women in Western countries, but in the vast United States there are still pockets of religious fanatics who in the name of purity do their best to keep the sexual thoughts and feelings of their girls from developing. Consider the case of Elissa Wall. Elissa had the misfortune to be born in 1986 to a family that belonged to the Fundamentalist Church of Jesus Christ of Latter-Day Saints, a break-away Mormon sect in the American Southwest that still practices polygamy. Her mother, who was also brought up in the Church's cloistered community, received no sex education and no preparation for marriage, apart from learning that women must always *keep sweet* and that they belonged to men, as she put it, *body, boots, and britches.* She had sixteen children with one man before being "reassigned" to another, who had fifteen other wives and dozens of children. When, at various points in her life, children of hers rebelled against the Church's strictures, she was ordered to cut off relations with them forever. And she complied, telling one of them, *I'd rather see you die than fight the priesthood.* Her greatest fear was not of the priesthood, though. It was of the out-side world, about which she knew nothing.

Elissa's fate seemed sealed. She was molested at the age of two, and her parents knew it. When she was fourteen, the Church's aging prophet had a reve-lation that she should marry a nineteen-year-old first cousin, whom she loathed. In her memoir there is a picture of Elissa on her wedding day, her face beet red from crying uncontrollably the night before. Totally unaware of sexual relations or how children are con-ceived, she resisted her husband on their wedding night. He, it turned out, was just as ignorant about sex as she was. Eventually he just raped her, after which she swallowed pills, hoping to kill herself. She became pregnant several times in the next few years, but mercifully miscarried every time.

The rest of Elissa's memoir is devoted to her escape and her brave and successful efforts to bring to justice the prophet's son, who was finally convicted of several crimes, among them rape and sexual assault of a child, and was given a life sentence in Texas. But the memoir is much more than a conventional prison break story. The unforgettable scenes are not those of cruelty and horror, though there are plenty of them. It is the scenes that evoke a stifling and, in the end, tyrannical ignorance that holds even the adults in its grip, creating an environment ideal for predators, who—adding to the perversity—are no more worldly than their victims.

Millions of adults around the world call themselves Christians. But can a Christian be an adult? It's a fair question. The world and its ways reveal themselves to any reader of the Hebrew Bible, which overflows with family sagas, *Bildungsromane*, and political intrigue. Adults marry, have children, educate them, cultivate land, seek and give counsel, get angry and are appeased, suffer and smite their enemies, get ill and die. There are good characters, evil characters, and many ambiguous ones like King David, who swings from sin to repentance and back again, like a pendulum. God, too, has his bad days, and the Hebrews never know quite what to expect from him. So they are forced to learn from experience and live with uncertainty. The characters of the Hebrew Bible mature before our eyes, and we mature psychologically and intellectually as we read about them.

Innocent lambs and children get more than their due in the Gospels, but we learn next to nothing about adult life. Christ first appears in the world as a child, yet a precocious one, with nothing to learn and no capacities in need of development. Mary says hardly a word, and Joseph doesn't speak at all (a thought-provoking omission). As for the disciples, we are told very little about their lives, not even about the extraordinary Judas, who seems to have strayed in from the Old Testament. Jesus does not prepare his disciples for carrying the burdens of adulthood in their families and communities. Instead he admonishes them, *If any one comes to me and does not hate his own father and mother and wife and children and brothers and sisters, yes, and even his own life, he cannot be my disciple.* Good disciples drop their nets and follow without asking questions. What their wives and children eat that night we are not told.

The early Christians were an apocalyptic sect that expected the Redeemer to return in their lifetime, so it made little sense for them to plan for their own future or that of their children. But the longer Christ's return was delayed, the more they had to accustom themselves to living in a world they thought they were just passing through. Discipleship turned out to be more complicated than preserving their innocence by imitating a lamb or being reborn as a child. It required a knowledge of life, of human nature, of political necessity. But their new scriptures did not confer this knowledge on them. Simple believers looked to the Gospels, then to the world, and the world looked back at them with a beatific smile. *Love your enemies . . . if anyone strikes you on the right cheek, turn to him the other also . . . take therefore no thought for the morrow: for the morrow shall take thought for the things of itself.* Brother Juniper had many ancestors.

> Behold, I send you forth as lambs among wolves.
> —Luke 10:3

No one who has read *Billy Budd: Sailor* will forget its innocent hero, or the demonic figure who brings about his death, the serpentine master-at-arms, John Claggart. Melville compares Billy to Adam, to a child, to a primitive, to the Lamb of God. Claggart, on the other hand, seems to have sprung from the imagination of Saint Augustine: he is possessed of an evil so radical that he dreams of killing Billy, *just because*. When Billy is first told of Claggart's hatred of him, he simply does not understand what he hears, the emotion is so alien to him. Which only enrages Claggart.

The story of their fateful encounter is structured like a Greek tragedy: in front of the ship's captain, Edward Fairfax Vere, Claggart falsely charges Billy with fomenting mutiny. Billy, astonished and tongue-tied, lashes out blindly, punching Claggart in the fore-head, killing him instantly. According to British military law, such a murder demands the death pen-alty. In a manner of hours, innocent Billy is strung up, though not before shouting, *God bless Captain Vere!*

Billy is right: poor Captain Vere needs God's help. While Melville's novella seems at first a simple Chris-tian morality tale about martyred innocence, it turns into a tragedy about the futility of innocence in polit-ical life. The action of the story takes place during the French Revolutionary Wars, and just before it begins, two major pro-Revolution mutinies had broken out on British ships and needed to be put down with arms. Vere was not trained to be a Solomon of the seas, to decide difficult moral cases involving others. He was appointed a naval officer to govern a warship in the midst of hostilities. He is a political actor, with-out the luxury of ignoring the consequences of his actions, and for such figures, achieving justice can be impossible. Billy was an innocent provoked to strike out, and on those grounds he should be exonerated, or his sentence reduced. Yet Vere has an obligation to see that regulations are enforced on his ship, as no one else will do it, and on those grounds Billy must hang. Besides, if Billy were exonerated, it might in-spire mutiny among the crew, who would sense a crack in the authority of the officers. And that might in turn scuttle the mission and possibly cost Britain the war. And so Billy is condemned by the tortured Vere, who dies in action not long afterward, muttering *Billy Budd! Billy Budd!*

In the Greek and even in the Hebrew tradition it is taken for granted that there is no prospect of perpetual peace on earth, given the nature of human beings and their societies. Conflict is inevitable in political affairs, genuine interests clash, power corrupts, ideology inebriates, and force and deception employed by the unjust must be met with force and deception employed by the just. There are wolves out there. It has been claimed that by refusing to accept this tragic vision complacently, the Christian moral revolution shifted the balance in favor of protecting innocent lambs, whose well-being must be our first concern, even in war. That is true. But it also bred the illusion that shepherds could afford to be innocents, too. Which was very good news for wolves.

> Where is the moral Switzerland we can
> emigrate to?
> —Uwe Johnson, *Anniversaries*

Innocence is central to the American political mythos. Since its inception the country has advertised itself as a radically new creation, brought into being in a self-conscious act of will after the Old World had botched history. This birth was also, in a deeper mythical sense, a rebirth, the return of Adam to Eden after millennia of exile. The idea that the human race was granted its second innocence at Plymouth Rock has coursed through American political rhetoric ever since the *Mayflower* landed there, and one sometimes still hears hollow evocations of it at election time. But with innocence comes fears of its loss, which are also embedded in the national mythos. The fear is that the further America moves beyond its original founding, the more it will adapt itself to the twilight world of raw power, uncertainty, and compromise, where every other nation lives. Like a perfectly innocent child, the nation will then find itself with each passing year *a stair lower from God*. Any backsliding into contaminating experience or tragic knowledge must therefore be resisted or removed from consciousness.

The Two Lambs Problem that plagues Christianity also plagues the United States in its dealings with the wider world. At certain historical junctures one has witnessed the optimistic, dewy-eyed version of American Christianity brought to bear on world politics, encouraging illusions about the benign motives of foreign adversaries, leading to an I-don't-want-to-know policy of isolationism. At others, the conviction that *darkness was upon the face of the deep* inspired thoughtless, self-righteous crusades using brute force to drive out the political infidels. Foreign nations have encountered both in their dealings with the United

States and, understandably, complain of hypocrisy. But the problem is much deeper. America has trouble imagining a role for itself that is not that of the Lamb of God, or that of the seven-headed beast of the Book of Revelation. And so it shuttles between them, leaving other nations to pay the price.

In the minds of many Americans, theirs is the Billy Budd of nations. In truth, they too often resemble Travis Bickle, the raging innocent in Martin Scorsese's *Taxi Driver*. A Vietnam veteran with scars on his back to prove it, Travis returns home in the 1970s and finds himself driving a cab in New York, where every street corner is a cross between *Vanity Fair* and the *Inferno*, strewn with garbage and men in super-fly outfits and women in hot pants looking for tricks. Travis wants to strike back somehow, but he doesn't know how. And so he writes himself into a chivalry tale, randomly choosing a teen prostitute as his reluctant damsel in distress and her two-bit pimp as his nemesis. Billy's deadly punch of Claggart was spontaneous, unrehearsed. Travis is a master of strategic planning worthy of a general's star. He chooses his weapons carefully; he eats right and works out; and every evening he prowls the ill-lit streets waiting for his chance to set the world back in simple order. One night this exterminating lamb finally accomplishes his mission, and blood splatters the camera lens.

> Their singleness, their ruthlessness, their one
> continuous wish makes the innocent bound to

be cruel, and to suffer cruelty. The innocent
are so few that two of them seldom meet—
when they do meet, their victims lie strewn
all round.

      —Elizabeth Bowen, *The Death of the Heart*

THE VERY RICH HOURS OF
SAMUEL PICKWICK, ESQ.

To be no longer innocent, but to wish that one
were, is part of the definition of an adult.
—W. H. Auden

Innocence is an illusion. We come into this world a
bundle of disordered drives and desires, some good,
some not. We are neither pure nor impure, we are
only somewhat educable. There is an art to transforming raw youths into decent mature adults, and its
tools are experience and knowledge. Some of it is
pleasant, some less so. And for every gain in knowledge of the world and mastery over ourselves, there
are corresponding losses—of spontaneity, trust,
transparency, immediacy, passion, simplicity, all the
things we associate with children. Such is life. We are
meant to leave the Garden and must reconcile ourselves to the chiaroscuro life beyond it.

Thus speaks the voice of experience, which has
held the floor throughout this chapter. And it must be
heard. But it also grates. There is something a little too
smug, a little too self-satisfied about those who parade
their lucidity and pat the heads of the benighted. Any
lesson, even a necessary one, can be learned too well.

There is a comfort in being disabused, a pride in turning up the lights and puncturing illusions that induces a different kind of blindness that needs to be challenged.

If the word *innocence* distorts human experience, we should abandon it. But do we really wish to rob ourselves of the characteristics and experiences the word denotes? Something quickens within when we see a child entranced by a mobile above the crib, or a graceful teen on a skateboard weaving through traffic, or blushing lovers, or a gratuitous act of kindness, or the simple craftsperson engaged in an intricate task he or she does well. These experiences fill us with wonder no less than the latest pictures of the universe from modern telescopes. The realist must face this reality, too. Innocence, in this sense, is not an illusion. We just have trouble integrating it into a mature view of life. It would seem a matter of great importance to learn whether one can acquire that view and still remain open to wonder.

This is the theme of Charles Dickens's beguiling, and underappreciated, first novel, *The Pickwick Papers*. As it opens, we find ourselves at a cheerful, alcohol-warmed meeting of the Pickwick Club, whose members have been honoring its founding president, who has just retired after a lucrative business career. After serious meditation on his future, Pickwick has decided to embark on a pseudoscientific tour around Britain, gathering stories, remarking geographical oddities, discovering forgotten buildings, and generally adding to the stock of our knowledge. His own stock of it, we soon learn, is not large, at least in dealing with others. He has never been married, has no children, and is possessed of a simple faith in human nature that renders him incapable of discerning duplicity. The Pickwick Club approves of their president's new venture, and several members, no more world-wise than he, decide to accompany him.

Unlike his innocent forefather, Don Quixote, who tilts at windmills and smashes his armor, Mr. Pickwick just moseys along, meeting jolly people and helping them out modestly when he can, receiving universal love in return. But then a serpent by the name of Jingle enters his garden. The sometime actor and full-time con artist has little trouble gaining Pickwick's confidence and eventually that of the family he is staying with. Within days of meeting them, Jingle has run off with one of the family's foolish spinster aunts in the hopes of getting his hands on her money. When he is caught, Jingle impudently demands to be paid off; Pickwick, the naïf, unable to imagine the scandal that publicity of this misadventure would provoke for the family, angrily objects as a matter of principle. But the patriarch, a man of the world, pays the scoundrel, and that is that. If there were lessons to be had from this episode—such as, don't trust everyone, or accept imperfect outcomes in an imperfect world—Mr. Pickwick stubbornly refuses to learn them and returns to his travels, his conscience clear.

But the comedy ends when he returns to London

for a short stay. An awkward conversation with his widowed landlady leaves the poor woman with the impression that Pickwick is proposing to her. When she is disabused of this notion, she feels somehow humiliated. And before long, after being hoodwinked by wolfish lawyers, she sues Mr. Pickwick for damages. All he would have to do, short of marrying her, is pay the amount, which he can afford, and the matter would be settled. But once again he stands on principle and naïvely entrusts his fate to the British courts. The case is called, Pickwick loses, and he finds himself condemned to the infamous Fleet Street debtors' prison in Central London.

Poor Pickwick. Nothing in his experience has prepared him for what he discovers there: whole families, whose only crime is bad luck, wasting away in filthy, airless cells, children starving, guards taking bribes, and prisoners stealing from one another. He was raised to be an English gentleman; his moral code is no more complex than *what's done* and *what's not done*. But what is to be done in the bowels of hell?

Fortunately, Pickwick has as his valet Sam Weller, a Cockney Sancho Panza who as a lad grew up on the hard streets of London and has gotten through life by never overestimating his fellow man. He is smitten with his master's moral beauty and knows that the poor man will be eaten alive in prison, so he contrives to have himself condemned to the Fleet as well, so he can serve his patron in loco parentis. Pickwick is moved. But more than that, he wants Sam to help him understand how people can be condemned to such conditions in civilized Britain. All Sam can think to answer is, *Lord bless your heart, sir, why, where were you half baptized?*

So experience once again comes to the rescue of innocence? Yes. But that's not all. True, Pickwick is eventually persuaded by Sam to pay his debt, and he leaves prison. But in another sense it is Pickwick who comes to Sam's rescue. While inspecting a room in the prison one day, Pickwick unexpectedly runs across the bounder Jingle and his servant, who had criss-crossed the country swindling people until they ran out of money and landed in the Fleet. Malnourished, dressed in rags, they have trouble making coherent speech. The cynical, supercilious Jingle bursts into genuine tears. And soon Pickwick does too. He then works behind the scenes to get the two men food, clothing, and clean linen in prison; next he pays their way out, arranges jobs for them in the West Indies, and takes care of their passage. When Sam learns of this, he is stunned into near silence, only able to mut-ter, *Well, I am damned!* over and over. Nothing in his experience has prepared him for such seemingly fool-ish behavior. Even more, nothing in his experience has prepared him to see such charity actually trans-form someone. As we learn at the end, Pickwick's generosity did pay off: before leaving, Jingle tells the older man, *You'll never repent it, Sir,* and at the end of the novel we learn that he and his servant have both become worthy members of society in the Caribbean, with no desire to return to Britain.

On leaving prison, Mr. Pickwick is no longer innocent or ignorant. His view of the world, and the evil in it, is now more complete, and he is grateful for *the enlargement of my mind* and *the improvement of my understanding.* But otherwise he is unchanged. He retires to the country along with Sam, helping him to get married and allowing him to live on the property. He watches over friends and their new families, spending much of his time attending christenings as godfather. Dickens assures us that *though somewhat infirm now, he retains all his former juvenility of spirit.*

It is Sam who becomes a different man. His worldliness is a pose acquired through rough experience, but a pose nonetheless. He has gotten comfortable in his assumption that, except for a few saints like Pickwick, human beings are always trying to take advantage of one another. As a realist, his guiding moral principle had been to put between his teeth any coin he received and test if it was real. This complacency arrested his knowledge of human nature, no less than Pickwick's naïveté had arrested his. And so they need each other. But of the two, Sam seems the greater beneficiary. Pickwick is unlikely to make the same mistakes that landed him in prison; he has become more aware of the world as it is. But he remains as curious, spontaneous, open to experience, and prepared for wonder as he ever was. Sam, on the other hand, becomes less cynical and therefore more realistic about the potentials of the human animal. The book is the story of his full baptism.

> Perhaps everybody has a Garden of Eden,
> I don't know; but they have scarcely seen their
> garden before they see the flaming sword.
> Then, perhaps, life only offers the choice of
> remembering the garden or forgetting it. Either,
> or; it takes strength to remember, it takes
> another kind of strength to forget, it takes a
> hero to do both. People who remember court
> madness through pain, the pain of the
> perpetually recurring death of their innocence;
> people who forget court another kind of
> madness, the madness of the denial of pain and
> the hatred of innocence; and the world is mostly
> divided between madmen who remember and
> madmen who forget. Heroes are rare.
> —James Baldwin, *Giovanni's Room*

The Once and the Now

ON NOSTALGIA

You will never be again
What you never were before.

—Theodor Storm

Every morning Odysseus sits on the beach and casts his eyes across the sun-flecked water. The breeze is fresh, and the waves rumble gently as they break. He is crying. For seven years since the end of the Trojan War he has been a prisoner in paradise, the unwilling consort of the beautiful nymph Calypso, who loves and fawns on him. Odysseus can't bear it. Since leaving Troy victorious, he has wandered the seas, hounded by the god Poseidon, who has prevented him from finding his way home to Ithaca. *Nothing is more sweet in the end than country and parents*, he laments. Eventually Zeus is driven to pity and orders Calypso to release him. Odysseus builds himself a raft, and after one last night of lovemaking and weeping, he sails off alone.

The home we return to is never the home we left. When Odysseus finally reaches Ithaca, Homer tells us, he learns that his estate has been occupied by suitors vying for the hand of his wife, Penelope, and dissipating his fortune while they wait. Odysseus comes to Penelope disguised as a beggar and kills the suitors. After he proves to her who he is, the couple goes to their bed, which Odysseus had made with his own hands, using a tall tree as one of the bedposts. They make love and fall asleep. There is no space between the two of them, between the couple and Odysseus's handiwork, between the bed and the tree, between the tree and the earth—all as if they sprang fully formed from the soil of Ithaca. Wholeness has been restored.

The fate of Aeneas, prince of Troy and adversary of Odysseus, was destined to be different. His home was no more, vanquished by the craven guile of the Greeks. As they poured from the belly of the wooden horse to destroy the city, Aeneas reached for his sword to resist. But in a vision the goddess Venus urged him to flee with the others, so he lifted his father onto his back and followed. As the ship made for open sea, he watched the flames consume everything he had ever known; then he turned his back on Troy forever. Odysseus would face worse deprivations than Aeneas did on his journeys, but the Greek knew that Ithaca still existed in time and space, and that hope for return was not vain. This balm was denied Aeneas. Only ashes littered the site of ancient Troy, and no Penelope awaited him.

The *Aeneid* is not about loss, however. It is a phoenix story about a reborn city that rises, quite literally, out of the flames. While on his journey Aeneas makes a stop at Delos to consult an oracle about his fate and receives an enigmatic reply: *The land of your ancestors will welcome you again, return to her generous breast. Seek out your ancient mother.* He is baffled.

But soon he has a dream in which the prophecy is confirmed: *Your home is elsewhere.*

That elsewhere will turn out to be Rome. The dream convinces Aeneas that his ancestors were originally from Italy, and not from Anatolia. By migrating to the former, Aeneas will in fact only be reclaiming what had been his people's rightful home in the past. And by building on the Tiber a magnificent new city outshining Troy, an invincible power prepared to conquer the world, Aeneas will also be turning the dial of time forward. Throughout his journey the gods confirm that this double movement—redeeming the past by leaping forward into the future—is his destiny. He is made to visit Hades and finds it crowded with Roman heroes of the future, who all look up to him as to a father. He is called to be the redeemer of his people, the link between what was and what will be. He accepts, and Virgil's poem then recounts in bloody detail how he conquered the local native tribes and, in the book's last lines, brutally killed a rebel leader who had come to surrender. *Yes*, he thinks, laying down his sword in extreme fatigue, *I have had my vision.*

THE FAMILY ALBUM

When you go looking for what is lost,
everything is a sign.

 　　　　　—Eudora Welty, "The Wide Net"

In the early seventeenth century, during the Wars of
Religion, European military officers began getting re-
ports of a recurring malady among their soldiers. The
symptoms: lack of appetite, weight loss, lethargy, in-
somnia, bouts of crying, in certain cases even halluci-
nations. The soldiers had trouble explaining why they
felt the way they did. But a pattern emerged: most of
the sufferers were mercenaries and impressed soldiers
fighting far from their native villages and countries.
More than a few Spaniards serving in Flanders came
down with this "heart illness" (*mal de corazón*) and
had to be sent back home. And for some reason it
particularly plagued the Swiss. Whenever one of them
sang or played the *ranz des vaches*, a traditional song
used to call the cows home, the others became incon-
solable. When the generals and colonels realized what
was happening, they banned the singing. But many
Swiss soldiers remained useless on the battlefield, so
they, too, had to be dismissed. They weren't cowards
or pacifists. All they needed was to see mountains and

fields again, smell country cooking, and drink fresh milk with their morning muesli. Once they returned to Switzerland, their symptoms disappeared. The cause of their nostalgia, like that of Odysseus, was spatial, as was its cure.

We think differently about nostalgia today. For us, the desire to return is temporal in nature, not spatial. What we ache to recover is a *world*, a previous state of affairs and the states of consciousness that accompanied them. Our nostalgia for childhood is not to squeeze our adult frame back into a high chair, it is to experience a state of mind unburdened by what we have experienced and learned since childhood and the responsibilities we have taken on. Our historical nostalgia has the same structure, extending to an entire social world, which we imagine was once simpler and happier. In truth, the nostalgic do not so much want to recover something as to lose something. They want to flee what to them tastes like toxic knowledge about the world and themselves. For this distaste there is no cure. Time is linear and irreversible, its arrow points relentlessly forward. We have no choice but to accept this. Yet we can't, not fully.

Nostalgia is a mood that mixes pleasure and pain in equal measure. Consider photographs. Ask parents why they take so many photos of their children, and they are likely to say that they want to preserve the memory of them at every stage of development so that one day they can look back and measure the time traversed. Photography is an exercise in anticipatory nostalgia. We foresee that, come a certain age, we will want to experience an odd pleasure that comes from reflecting on what has been lost. Yet how to describe the flood of feelings set off by seeing all those pictures? There are the simple pleasures of self-recognition, of recalling happiness and pride, of seeing life as a continuum. There is also bitter with the sweet. Baby pictures bring out longing for a time when the child was an innocent wonder and regret over not having appreciated how fleeting the moment would be. It is a pain that the arrival of grandchildren only partially relieves. Vacation pictures remind us, or delude us into thinking, that family relations were once simpler and happier than they are now. We see ourselves, thinner and with more hair, looking carefree as we cradle the nursing baby or put our arms around wet, shivering, reluctant teenagers on a beach. This brings pain, then pleasure in the pain. There is something mildly masochistic about the family album.

Do we as individuals really want to return to the past conjured up by the images? In the end, no. Whenever we've tried to relive moments from the past, we've almost always experienced disappointment. The old neighborhood we visit looks shabby and dull. The ex-lover we invite for a drink does, too. Psychologists suggest that suffering nostalgics do not really want to possess the lost object, they only want to preserve the bittersweet desire for it. Actually retrieving it or accepting its loss would rob them of a feeling they have structured their lives around. They are stuck, and their resistance to getting unstuck is tenacious, since it would force them to confront the open horizon before them. Freud developed a psychotherapy to free people of that fear. No such therapy has yet been found for nostalgic societies.

Nations and peoples fall into nostalgic moods just as individuals do. It is hard to think of societies that don't romanticize their origins. The myths they conjure up combine childlike innocence and martial grandeur in varying proportions. *Once we were simple and pure! Once we were strong!* Or, most powerfully of all, *Once we were strong because we were simple and pure!* Yet the parallel between individual and collective nostalgia takes us only so far. No matter how much I embellish my memories and force them into neat narratives to make sense of myself, the experiences I remember are my own, not someone else's. The firsthand memory of nations does not extend further back than a single human life span, less than a century. Every literate society's image of its past is necessarily mediated by embellished accounts handed down over the years, even millennia, and modified at each step. Or by retrospective attempts to reconstruct events and past psychological experience from shards that we in the present deem to be significant. All history is pastiche. In preliterate societies, collective memories from the distant past are embedded in rituals; they are remembered by being reenacted, not read. Literate societies remember through articulate myths and narratives whose secondhand, constructed nature has to be veiled if the stories are to hold their power.

It is always surprising to learn that an ancient tradition is not so ancient after all. Two amusing examples happen to concern the Scots. In the mid-eighteenth century a poet of some talent named James Macpherson published what he claimed to be the English translation of fragments of an ancient Gaelic epic. It had been composed, he asserted, by a mysterious blind bard of the third century CE named Ossian, the Homer of the Scottish Highlands—a lie that appealed to the proto-Romantic mood of European letters at the time. The poems, which Macpherson seems to have written by drawing from Irish poem cycles, were welcomed not only by his fellow nationalists but also by some of the greatest thinkers and poets of the age, including Goethe, who placed translated fragments of Ossian in one of his works. From the start, doubts were raised about the epic's authenticity. Samuel Johnson, when asked whether he thought any man from the present age could have written it, replied, *Yes, sir, many men, many women, and many children.* Macpherson never produced the Gaelic manuscripts he claimed to have translated. Still, the poem continued to be read and translated throughout the nineteenth century, feeding nostalgia across Europe for a pre-imperial, pre-industrial age.

Another symbol of Scotland's heroic age, the clan

kilt, has little more foundation in history than do the Ossian poems. There is no evidence of distinctive Highland dress before the sixteenth century, when Scots typically wore a long shirt covered by a belted cloak, sometimes made of murky tartan. The skirt we now call the kilt was in fact invented in the eighteenth century by an English Quaker, a manufacturer who wished his scantily clad Scottish factory workers to be properly dressed. The garment experienced some popularity among workers until it was banned by the British after the rebellion of 1745. Not until the English ban was lifted in 1782 did the kilt become a nationalist badge of honor, worn mainly by gentry wishing to play up their real or imagined Highland roots. After the Napoleonic Wars, during which the Scottish kilt was observed by armies across Europe, it was extolled by Romantics fascinated with noble primitives, which is what they considered the Highlanders to be. Only thereafter did distinctive plaids become associated with clans, thanks to the marketing genius of a clothing manufacturer who developed his own fanciful pattern book, arbitrarily assigning this or that tartan to particular clans.

The practice continues to this day. In 2016 a Scottish rabbi registered a "kosher Jewish tartan" with the official Register of Tartans, which itself had only been established in 2008. The pattern has gold to represent the Ark of the Covenant, silver to represent the Torah, and blue and white to represent the Israeli flag. It now festoons kilts, neckties, yarmulkes, and golf balls.

ABOUT FACE

The rule is, jam tomorrow and jam
yesterday—but never jam today.
—Lewis Carroll, *Through the Looking Glass*

Nostalgia can sometimes be enjoyable. Anyone with a good internet connection can now research their lineage themselves or with the help of very profitable businesses that promise an ancestry worth celebrating. But when an entire nation or people or faith begins searching for lost time, darker emotions and fantasies emerge. Political nostalgia transforms a feeling that *things are not as they should be* into the conviction that *things are not what they once were*. Everything hangs on that *once*. Once we were innocent and pure, now we are not. Once we were kings, now we are prisoners. Once we lived in Eden, now we live in Los Angeles or Cairo or Dubai. Once we were nigh unto gods, now we must grovel for assistance.

There is a trap hidden in that *once*. The more we dream about a lost Eden, the less bearable the present feels, and this feeling then inclines us to yearn even more for what we imagine we have lost. Soon we become incapable of seeing the world as it presents itself to us without the shadows of an imagined past cast upon it. Political nostalgics are sick with history itself. They see themselves as victims of a cataclysm that has stranded them in the present, a foreign country. Some become paralyzed, incapable of taking nourishment from what life still offers, and begin to waste away. Or they feel the coffin closing and panic; adrenaline races to their hearts, and they become capable of anything. The original philosophical question—*how should I live?*—has little meaning for them. *When to live?*—that is the question. And *Now* is not an acceptable answer.

There are many versions of the myth of the Golden Age. The one told by the ancient Greek poet Hesiod is the most familiar to us. Frustrated by his lazy, shiftless brother Perses, Hesiod wrote a poem to explain to him why human beings had to work. He described a divinely created golden race that once lived off of the fruit of the earth without toil. But when this race disappeared, and each subsequent one was fatally flawed in some way, we ended up in the age of iron, where we must now make our home. For us, life is toil and suffering, and so it will remain until our destruction. That end is inevitable but can be postponed if we are decent, law-abiding, and respectful of the gods. Hesiod does not dangle before his brother any hope of returning to the Golden Age or of entering a new one. His message: back to the plow.

In the Book of Genesis, the Hebrew Bible teaches a similar moral lesson by different means. The Jewish tradition does not, as Christianity does, treat the drama in Eden as marking a fall in human nature it-self, a transformation from innocence to sinfulness. It interprets the story symbolically to explain why the world as God created it was and is good—and why nonetheless we are destined to toil and suffer depriva-tions in it. Longing for a return to Eden is explicitly rejected. Sensing perhaps what a psychological drug nostalgia can be, the rabbis closed the door on our beginnings. If the Hebrew Bible has a theory of decline and loss, it is, so to speak, a vertical one: Israel rises or falls, is exiled or returns, depending on whether or not it freely chooses to abide by God's covenant. What happens on the horizontal plane of history is just a chronicle of that covenant relationship. One can al-ways rise spiritually to God; one can never find him by moving backward in time. When the Messiah brings redemption is his business; how we live until then is our business.

The modern historical imagination is not terribly drawn to moral parables like this one; instead it is subject to the entwined emotions of hope in the hu-man future and nostalgia for the human past. No sooner had poets and thinkers in the Renaissance an-nounced the rebirth of ancient learning than their ad-versaries began idealizing the older darkness. It is remarkable how quickly nostalgia for the Middle Ages grew up in Europe after they ended. Already in the seventeenth century there was a vast literature, parodied by Cervantes in *Don Quixote*, that extolled the medieval chivalric virtues of simplicity and valor, which stood in contrast to the new, bourgeois spirit of gain and the terrifying impersonal mechanization of warfare. By the nineteenth century, Romantics like John Ruskin were stoking a passion for Gothic architecture and the ruins of Catholic Europe, and encouraging architects to return to the old forms. The more the nineteenth century progressed in science, industry, and even politics, the more nostalgic it became in spirit. Such are the hydraulics of historical consciousness.

> Who knows whether in a couple of centuries there may not exist universities for restoring the old ignorance?
>
> —Georg Christoph Lichtenberg

But nostalgia can also be provoked by failure to make progress. Collective shame is among the most powerful and least appreciated of the psychological forces driving historical change. Herodotus would not have been surprised to learn how significantly it has shaped global history in the modern era, since it did so in the ancient world as well. Feelings of inferiority can haunt any society. Even powerful empires can live with chips on their shoulders, even the greatest of all, Rome.

Rome grew from a small city into an extensive

empire within a cultural arena first dominated by the Greeks. Religion, art, architecture, literature, philosophy, the sciences—in all these domains Romans were initially conscious of their belatedness and inferiority. When individuals feel themselves to be inferior in a particular social setting, they tend to do one of two things: either they try to "pass" as being like others in the group, or they react to rejection (real or imagined) and assert their difference, which becomes a compensatory form of superiority. Until Rome conquered Greece militarily and forged a hybrid culture of its own, Roman elites were divided about how to respond to Greek achievements. Many had Greek masters educate their children, knowing that their status in society would depend partly on how well they spoke the language and mastered the literature. Their palaces were full of marble copies of Greek bronze sculptures, and they listened to Greek poetry while reclining on couches. But some chafed against what they saw as Greek arrogance, and asserted pride in things they felt distinguished them from their rivals. Romans, they told themselves, are simple and direct, not slippery and refined like the Hellenes. They are doers, not talkers; honest, not treacherous; courageous, not cowardly; tanned and strong, not pale and weak. In a word, Roman-ness (*Romanitas*) was the pinnacle of human virtue, and everything that came from the Greeks carried a disease (*morbus Graecus*).

That is something of an exaggeration, but it does capture a cultural mood that historians like Tacitus expressed when contrasting the idealized virtues of the republican era with the cravenness and moral decadence of the imperial age. When in this mood, Romans were visited by the specter of decline, always worrying that their vital essence was being sapped or had already disappeared. Already in the late republican period, when Roman power was rapidly expanding, nostalgic patricians like Cato the Elder were railing against the effects of luxury, declaring that Rome was losing its rustic virility and becoming effeminate. He was especially obsessed with Greek philosophers, who were gaining a following among Roman youth at the time. When a group of philosophers visited Rome, the famous skeptic Carneades was among them, and he is said to have delivered two speeches, one in praise of justice, the other against it. Cato immediately perceived a threat to civic virtue in this moral skepticism and began making speeches against philosophy as such, denouncing Socrates as a chatterbox who attacked the laws and customs of Athens as a prelude to making himself tyrant. Before the Senate, Cato declared that Rome would lose its empire if its youth were allowed to study the subject, and eventually he persuaded his colleagues to banish the visiting philosophers and have them transported back to Athens.

Rome's experience with Greece eventually became a global psychological experience. Beginning in the eighteenth century, owing to trade and then colonialism, and today with air travel and the internet, non-

Western countries and cultures have had no choice but to confront the modern West as idea and reality, and simultaneously to confront themselves. Russia was an extraordinary theater for this kind of drama. Well before Napoleon tempted fate by marching on Moscow, Russia had felt itself invaded by the West. Ideas associated with the Enlightenment were first introduced by Peter the Great and inspired his radical—and much resented—reforms. Catherine the Great, who cultivated personal relations with the French *philosophes*, only pushed those reforms further. The elite, now French-speaking, embraced these ideas and began educating their children along modern European lines, much as the Romans sent theirs to Greek tutors. And, as in Rome, an intellectual and political reaction to these changes set in.

In the great novels of Turgenev and Dostoyevsky we are witness to clashes between modernizers and antimodernizers, Westernizers and chauvinists, atheists and neoorthodox Slavophiles, fathers and sons. The Russians were first to go through a political-intellectual cycle that has become familiar elsewhere in the world: a nation or culture encounters the modern West and, at first, feels backward and humiliated, so begins to slavishly imitate its ways. When the expected benefits of modernization do not materialize—or when they do, with unpalatable consequences—the new knowledge suddenly appears poisoned and is resisted. At that moment there arises from the depths of the imagination the idea of returning to a simpler past unburdened by this knowledge. Our problem, the thought goes, is not that we have always been backward. It is that we no longer have the determination and confidence we once did to defend our strengths. This thought then inspires ideological movements promising to restore a lost greatness, to lead the way back home.

The Slavophiles were one such movement, or family of movements. The questions they asked were not foolish ones, quite the contrary. What will happen to religious faith if we modernize? How can traditional authority be maintained? Will common decency and fellow feeling die out? And art as well? For the Slavophiles, modernization meant the destruction of all that was virtuous and noble in the traditional Russian way of life. But like so many nostalgic political activists, they had trouble distinguishing the modern innovations themselves from the Western countries that had brought them to Russia. They were incapable of seeing modernization as a general historical process that only happened to begin in the West and was at first directed against traditional life there as well. Instead the Slavophiles convinced themselves that modernization was the fullest realization of a distinctive Western culture and all that was wrong with it. The struggle they saw was not between premodern and modern life everywhere; it was between the West and the rest. Their writings endlessly repeat the same refrain: the Western *mind* is rigid, abstract, rationalistic, and so fixated on the future that it destroys life in the present, while the Russian *soul* and *heart* are authentic, charitable, and devout; they bring everything into harmony. These impassioned words from Ivan Kireevsky, a leading Slavophile, are typical:

> In the West, theology became a matter of rationalistic abstraction, whereas in the Orthodox world, it retained its inner wholeness of spirit. In the West, the forces of reason were split asunder, while here there was a striving to maintain a living totality . . . In the West, pagan and Christian civilization grew into one another, while here there was a constant effort to keep the truth pure . . . In the West we find a dichotomy of the spirit, a dichotomy of thought, a dichotomy of learning, a dichotomy of the state, a dichotomy of estates, a dichotomy of society, a dichotomy of familial rights and duties, a dichotomy of morals and emotions . . . We find in Russia, in contrast, a predominant striving for wholeness of being, both external and inner, social and individual, intellectual and workaday, artificial and moral.

The same nostalgic tropes litter the literature of contemporary political Islamism, which purports to explain *the obvious incongruity between the Once and the Now*, as one revered thinker put it. The Muslim world's encounter with the modernizing West was in many ways more shocking and destabilizing than was Russia's. For centuries after its founding Islam dominated Christendom militarily and culturally, so there was understandably little reason for Muslims to be curious about a backward people. (The West did not invent cultural snobbery.) It was only after the decisive defeat of Ottoman forces at the end of the seventeenth century, and then Europe's scientific and technological takeoff, that educated Muslims began to pay more serious attention. Ambassadors and their educated scribes who visited Europe started writing travelogues about their journeys, some critical, others slightly admiring. They expressed conflicting emotions. There was shame in the fact that a civilization that once cultivated great mathematicians and astronomers no longer did, and that Muslims were not even aware of fundamental European advances. There was fascination with the shocking spectacle of European parliamentary politics, which had no equivalent in the Muslim world. And there was a kind of anxious puzzlement about the social and sexual mixing made possible by the modern city. As in Russia, educated Muslim opinion in the nineteenth century was divided between proponents of Western-style modernization, opponents who defended Islamic tradition, and compromisers who thought they could have both.

But a different sort of fundamentalist movement also developed, one that rejected both modernization and existing Islamic practice and learning. Their leading thinkers held that the religious tradition had been corrupted quite early in its history by worldly political ambitions, luxury, leisure, and (again) philosophy. The task for pious Muslims today, therefore, was to renew Islam from within by looking back to the very first century of the faith, to the age of the Four Rightly Guided Caliphs. And to connect that *once* with the *now*, these fundamentalist thinkers confected an intellectual lineage for themselves running back, very selectively, to medieval forefathers, the so-called *Salaf*, whom they imagined to be like themselves, standing against the religious decadence of their time and the infiltration of alien ideas, and calling Muslims back to the Golden Age. Many of these modern Salafists had little to no scholarly training in the traditions of Islamic legal and Koranic interpretation stretching back over a millennium and the debates carried out by the rival schools. They relied heavily on the seemingly more transparent sayings of Muhammad that were preserved in the oral tradition, which are more open to fanciful, and certainly inflexible, readings. The most influential among them had begun as secular intellectuals—writers, journalists, teachers, engineers—and were more familiar with modern political disputes than with medieval theological ones. They lived in and spoke to the present. But by discovering the lost tradition, they could now do so in the charged language of history.

Give someone a set of political principles, and he will need to understand them before acting. Give someone a history, a story that elicits anger and pride, hope and courage, and you have instantly made a soldier. The modern Salafists understood this, and so have the different streams of radical Islamism that developed later in the twentieth century. Their political literature relies heavily on stories rather than theological reasoning. It is transparently nostalgic, eminently accessible, and aimed at uplift. The basic structure of the historical narrative it develops is little different from that of the Slavophiles and other nineteenth-century Romantic nationalists. There was a period of original goodness and simplicity in which we were strong and lived harmoniously; that period was brought to an end by a departure from tradition; fascination with an alien way of life and poisoned Western knowledge then alienated us further from our true selves; and all this explains our current misery. The narrative then becomes a prophecy. It identifies a saving remnant that retained a memory of tradition and will redeem the nation and restore its strength by expelling what is alien and overrefined and returning to the old ways. All other options have been tried, and all have failed. We are at a crossroads. The time to act is now. *Will you join us, friend?*

Dostoyevsky was convinced that the sources of nihilism were godlessness and a willingness to make any sacrifice, no matter how immoral, in the name of the future. One can only speculate what he would have made of modern jihadism, which pretends to speak for God and is willing to make any sacrifice, but in the name of the past. He surely would have been intrigued by a figure like Ahlam al-Nasr, a female jihadist writer who has been called "the Poetess of the Islamic State" and writes books with titles like *The Blaze of Truth*. In 2015 al-Nasr moved to Raqqa, then the capital of the caliphate of the Islamic State in Syria, in order to be closer to the divine action. In 2016 an American magazine published a profile of her that ended with these sentences:

> In her Raqqa diary, Ahlam al-Nasr describes the ISIS capital as a place of everyday miracles, a city where believers can go to be born again into the old, authentic faith. In the caliphate, she writes, "there are many things we've never experienced except in our history books."

Odysseus has landed.

CIVIS ROMANUS SUM

For who can doubt that Rome would rise again
instantly if she began to know herself?
—Petrarch

It would have been easier to build Rome in a
day than Athens.
—Ernst Bloch

The nostalgic have trouble bearing the news that the
present is happening, and soon will have happened,
and that they will be obliged to drag it with them like
an embarrassing sibling as they make their way forward in time. They dream of being free, utterly free,
from this *now*. Some flee it by imagining heading
back to an unrecoverable past. Another sort flees,
paradoxically, into the future.

To the apocalyptic mind, historical time is not continuous. It is a surface that suffers rips and tears and
is pocked with chasms left by earthquakes. Such an
outlook can induce historical despair, as it does in
backward-looking nostalgics who keep searching for
a bridge back to the other side. But it can also generate
hope. If history is subject to cataclysms that shift the
arrow of time in a new direction, the thought occurs

that in willfully creating another cataclysm, one might regain control over time, redirect the arrow, and set things aright. For the forward-looking nostalgic, the lostness of the past becomes a source of inspiration, even a recruiting tool for building a future inspired by what once was. Those in the grip of this passion imagine themselves to be like Aeneas, heading out to sea while Troy smolders behind them. It may not be possible for our civilization to return to its blessed infancy, but it can be rejuvenated. Rebirth, not return, is their goal.

The ideologies of modern fascism are all heirs to the *Aeneid*, and in more ways than one. Virgil's poem provided a historical schema for giving the present both meaning and a mission, specifically to bring about a civilizational repetition. It also is an example of how intellectuals can serve as instruments of whatever power is trying to bring a repetition about. Quite apart from the poet's literary achievement, his epic is a masterpiece of propaganda, subtly drawing the reader into an adventure story derived from older myths, which little by little becomes a certificate of legitimate birth for the new Roman order inaugurated by Julius Caesar and Emperor Augustus. Modern scholars see traces of dissent in the poem, but its influence was owed entirely to its patriotic idealization of *Romanitas*.

That fascism was born in modern Italy may have been happenstance, but the inescapable presence of the classical past there certainly made it easier for

Mussolini and his followers to point to the grandeur
that was, and would be again. Despite his *opera buffa*
comportment, Mussolini was an inspired visionary
who intuited the ways in which ancient myth could be
exploited to galvanize industrial workers and convince them that the future they were fighting for had
been foreshadowed in the past. His revolutionary nostalgia was in every sense postmodern: it rebelled
equally against remnants of the Old Regime that still
retained their force in Italy, and against the supposed
exploitative modern alliance of parliamentary democracy and industrial capitalism. His March on Rome
in 1922 conjured up both an ancient Roman tradition
of Rubicon crossing and a modern French one of mass
popular uprisings. Fascist propaganda portrayed him
as the guarantor of the Italian future and as the re-
incarnation of Caesar and Augustus. He knew how to
play the part:

> The Rome that we contemplate with pleasure
> and are preparing is not about the stones of
> the past, but a difficult preparation for the fu-
> ture. Rome is our point of departure and point
> of reference. It is our symbol . . . *Civis roma-
> nus sum.*

I am a Roman citizen. So, apparently, were Mussolini's followers in their own eyes. In 1937–38 the regime
celebrated the two thousandth anniversary of the birth
of Emperor Augustus, and an Augustan Exhibition of

Romanità was organized that was attended by hundreds of thousands of Italians.

The German Nazis had no Coliseum or Roman Forum to serve as backdrop to their rallies. They borrowed something else from Rome, a book—*Germania*, by Tacitus. It is a sort of anthropological field report on Germany that the historian wrote at the end of the first century CE, an odd work to have inspired nostalgic reveries. Tacitus, it seems, never once set foot in Germany. His account, drawn from various sources, including Caesar's memoirs, appears to have been written largely for contemporary polemical purposes. Tacitus deplored the decadence of the Empire, which he later evoked so vividly in his *Annals* and *Histories*, and *Germania* appears to be an early, veiled attempt to criticize it by appealing to primitivism. In the book one discovers a strong, rustic people resembling the ancient Latins of lore: rude, truthful, loyal, united, proud, belligerent. They knew neither luxury nor adultery. Encouraged by women baring their breasts, men marched off into battle, singing, indifferent to cold and hunger. And any man who had not killed an enemy had to go unshaven and wear a ring in his nose as signs of his shame. These Teutons could not be more different from imperial Romans, which was Tacitus's point. Over the centuries *Germania* became a reference for writers in many countries who condemned the decadence of their time, and it contains many of the commonplaces about noble savages that one finds throughout subsequent European literature. The book became particularly popular in German lands after Luther translated it, no doubt to contrast the corruptions of papal Rome with the simple piety of the primitive Church.

Luther's translation also became a key source for volkish thinkers of the nineteenth century who wanted to protect the earthy culture of rural Germany from the decadent bourgeois culture being imported from effeminate France. They quoted approvingly Tacitus's report that the Teutons practiced a brutal justice, killing slaves if they seriously disobeyed, drowning traitors and deserters in the swamps, and in some cases practicing human sacrifice. But one sentence in particular drew their attention. It is where Tacitus says, in passing, *I accept the view of those who think that the peoples of Germania have never been tainted by intermarriage with other nations, and stand out as a race distinctive, pure and unique of its kind.* He goes on to describe them as blue-eyed and ruddy haired, with immensely strong bodies that could bear severe cold and hunger. The modern racial "theorists" had found their urtext. Just as Rome was supposedly weakened and collapsed owing to racial mixing with the peoples it conquered, so Germany was threatened by mixing with alien races and cultures, particularly the Jews. This is how *Germania* became, in the words of one Nazi propagandist, *a bible that every thinking German should possess, as this booklet by the Roman patriot fills us with pride in our forefathers' superior character.*

For a backward-looking nostalgic like Heinrich Himmler, Tacitus's portrayal of racially pure, belligerent Teutons in their dark forests provided sufficient mythological inspiration for the Nazi policy of national rejuvenation through extermination. For Hitler, it did not. While he recognized the usefulness of volkish propaganda, he also understood that idealizing such an undeveloped culture would distract Germans' attention from the glistening new Rome they were capable of building. As he had already complained in *Mein Kampf* in the 1920s, the imagination of many of his dreamy early followers—meeting in the back rooms of seedy taverns, clad in lederhosen—didn't extend beyond the romance of conservative villages nestled in Bavarian valleys. Hitler wanted to create an empire that would be mentioned by posterity in the same breath as those of classical antiquity and would be remembered equally for its military conquests and its cultural achievements. To awaken this ambition, he had to find a way to connect Walhalla with the agora, the fur-clad Germans with the toga-clad Greeks. And he found it in the racial theory of the Aryan people.

The term *Aryan* was first adopted by Western linguists in the late eighteenth century to describe a family of Indo-European languages, not a race or a people. But in the nineteenth century, when Romantic nationalism was at its peak, European scholars, and especially pseudo-scholars, began to speculate about the existence of an actual Aryan ur-race. And as the century progressed, that speculation became for many a scientific certainty that was used across Europe and the Americas to justify slavery, colonialism, anti-Semitism, and much else.

In its original form, Aryan race theory suggested that all the European peoples—the French, Germans, English, Spanish, Italian, Hungarians, and more—had a common ancestry, and so in racial terms were fundamentally equal. Nazi race theorists came up with an imaginative, and in the end deadly, variation of this idea. They argued, on the basis of no evidence whatsoever, that the original Aryans had not spread out in the distant past from the Indus Valley into Europe, as the theory required. Rather, just as Aeneas had discovered that the Trojans were originally from Italy, so these "scientists" claimed to have discovered that the Aryans' original home was actually in the German forests (though one dissenting Nazi scholar insisted it was near the port city of Lübeck). In this rewriting of the modern myth, the Aryans subsequently spread out from Germany into the rest of Europe and thence into India, and then back again—not the other way around. The Nazi regime invested enormous energy into propagating this myth and, through its team of archaeologists in the SS, supported pseudo-academic research in history and anthropology to demonstrate its truth. This is how Hitler put it in a speech from 1933:

> Greeks and Romans become so close to the
> Germans because the latter have sought their
> roots in a founding race, and thus by force of
> attraction the immortal achievements of the
> ancients are repeated by its racial descendants.

Once this Aryan racial link was made, the full
range of symbols from the ancient world lay at the
service of Nazi propaganda officials. All the cultural
achievements of the ancient world could now be
claimed as German, and all the military achievements
of Rome as well. Pericles was blue-eyed, Augustus
blond. Hitler declared Sparta to have been the first
racist state, and sycophantic Nazi scholars called them
the Prussians of antiquity. In 1933 the race-obsessed
German philosopher Alfred Bäumler gave a lecture in
Berlin, "Against the Un-German Spirit," in which he
contrasted the manly political education of the Spar-
tans, aimed at forming citizen-soldiers, with the effeminate, Jew-infected democratic education of the
Weimar Republic. He then called on his student audience, many in SS uniforms, to take the first step toward restoring the Spartan spirit by destroying all
books that were poisoning the German soul. One can
easily find documentary footage of what happened
next: twenty thousand volumes were taken from the
library and fed to the flames in the university's court-
yard, to the amusement of those whose faces were illuminated by the fire. The devil's bride had once again
been driven from German soil.

THE WRINKLED CHILD

> The god of Regret and Nostalgia is a child with
> an old man's face.
>> —Antonio Tabucchi, *Woman of Porto Pim*

There are those who have earned their nostalgia all
too well. One thinks of exiles, migrants, victims of
war and natural disasters, all those who have lost a
home and cannot expect the recompenses of Odysseus
or Aeneid. Their loss is double. The chain of memories
that constitutes the self, and is reinforced by the familiar, has been broken. So has their confidence that the
world will ever make a place for them. Now all the
smells are unfamiliar and somehow menacing; the
food makes their stomachs rumble; hearing a forgotten song brings them to tears. But unlike the Swiss
soldiers who returned to their mountain villages when
they could no longer fight, the displaced cannot help
but keep an anxious eye on the horizon, their inner
luggage always packed. Half out fear, half out of hope.

One of the ironies of modern living is that the
ideal of *a better future* can induce an ache for the past
in anyone. The creative destruction that brings us ever
flatter liquid-crystal television screens flattens and
liquifies everything else in its path. The Maoist dream

of permanent revolution is finally being realized—in politics, economics, technology, science, medicine, culture, family life, intimate relations, and personal identity. There is nothing new about passing through a historical period, even a very long one, of great disruption. What is new in the last half century is the nagging sense that accelerating disruption has become a permanent condition of human life—that to be human is no longer to plant oneself in the earth as Odysseus did, but to surf on a choppy sea and struggle desperately to stay upright. The shock of the new has been replaced by the shock of the ephemeral. Even if material and social conditions of life improve over time, those improvements cannot but seem just as improvised and tentative as what preceded them. All this can leave us feeling like exiles without our having crossed a single border, without even walking out the front door. But how to adjust? We know that a failure to mourn a single loss can wreak havoc on an individual's psyche. We have no idea what it means to mourn when we wake up every morning in a different Potemkin village. That reactionary politics are flourishing in our liquid world should surprise no one.

Historical nostalgia is a peculiar manifestation of the will to ignorance. It is a failure to accept and mourn the loss of a world that sufferers have never had direct experience with. That world must first be conjured up in the imagination before it can just as imaginatively be made to disappear. This imagined world need not be invented out of whole cloth; it can be patched together rather convincingly from genuine traces of the past, selectively chosen. Once planted in the imagination, it can then serve the nostalgic mind as a measure by which selectively chosen present experiences can be gauged. In this game the present will always be found wanting. When encountering an antiquarian soul in the grip of this resistance to full knowledge of the past and present, one often cannot help feeling that some other loss, too painful to avow, has been transferred onto the world stage as a battle that can be choreographed and repeatedly restaged, as with little toy soldiers. *The possession of ancestral furniture changes its meaning in such a soul*, Nietzsche once remarked, *for the soul is rather possessed by the furniture.* And so they devote their lives to seeking a Troy they will never find. They wander erratically in the desert, tentless nomads chasing mirages, sunburned and shivering in the night.

> When a belief vanishes, there survives it . . . a
> fetishistic attachment to the old things which it
> did once animate, as if it was in them and not
> in ourselves that the divine spark resided, and
> as if our present incredulity had a contingent
> cause—the death of the gods.
>
> —Marcel Proust, *Swann's Way*

Envoi

"Light, light, more light!" they tell us that the dying Goethe cried. No, warmth, warmth, more warmth!, for we die of cold and not darkness. It is not the night that kills, but the frost.

—Miguel de Unamuno

Our young friend who returned to the cave has been settled in for some time now. He doesn't remember his brief experience in the sun, and given the power of the machine enveloping his head once again, buried memories of it are unlikely to resurface. He feels warm, he jokes and plays with his virtual friends again, he sees the stars, and at night he dreams of fantastic, improbable adventures in which he emerges victorious and loved. The unexamined life suits him just fine.

His was a special case, though. Unlike the rest of us, who live in uncertainty about what knowledge might or might not mean for our lives, after leaving the cave and its ever-changing illusions he was placed before a fait accompli: *this is what is, it will never be different, love it or leave it.* And so he left it. We, on the other hand, must anticipate the effects of confronting truth, which is why, over time, most of us develop a basic disposition toward seeking it. At one extreme, there is the person who treats his life as a journey of discovery, expecting pleasure and happiness from it—

homo viator. At the other, there is the person who anticipates loss and harm, and so builds dikes against the tides and flees if the waters crest over the top— *homo fugiens.* Two human types, two ways of living for us to choose between.

How easy the choice sounds, put that way. But there is nothing easy about determining our basic orientation in life, to the extent that we ever self-consciously can. The hardest part is just that: becoming conscious of ourselves as creatures whose wills to know and not to know are always in play. There is no knowing without feeling, and certainly no resistance to knowing without feeling. Plato understood this more deeply than any philosopher. The Socrates he portrays is a great seducer who cannot engage in the search for truth with his friends until he inspires them emotionally to join in the adventure. And so he does his best to make himself lovable in their eyes as a fearless explorer whose courage they try, and usually fail, to match. As he lay dying, those friends wept uncontrollably—an irrational response, he tells them, since what matters is how one lives, not what happens after death. This was his parting gift, an argument less convincing than emotionally benevolent.

We all want to think of ourselves as courageous and open to experience, as seizing life rather than being buffeted by it. Who would want to look in the mirror and see himself working hard to maintain a false picture of the world, hiding evidence from himself and patching the inner tube of his beliefs to keep the bicycle of his commitments rolling? Stated this way, none of us. And yet people do.

That is why, at the end of these rambles, I feel obliged to warn the reader against forming any simple, self-congratulatory judgments about *homo fugiens* as being somehow alien to ourselves. We have seen just what a powerful and destructive force the will to ignorance can be, and we need only pick up a work of history or look out the window to confirm what we have learned. This book happens to appear in the middle of a perfect storm, when different manifestations of the resistance to knowledge have combined to create ideological winds that batter us. One doesn't have to search far today to run into misologues who reject reasoning as a fool's game that only cloaks the real machinations of power. Or bagpipes who believe they have been blessed with private access to truth and have been chosen to make sure we live in the light of it. Or mass movements made up of holy fools and eternal children whose distaste for the present sends them rushing, vainly, to restore an imagined past. Nor is it hard to find today's prophets of ignorance, those learned despisers of learning who, whether from conviction or ambition, idealize people who resist doubt and build ramparts around their fixed beliefs. In the face of all this, those devoted to reasoning and open inquiry can start to feel like refugees.

But we must never forget the lesson of Oedipus

with which we began: that the urges to confront or to flee the truth are present in all of us. The harder the truth, the greater the temptation to escape it. Just consider the very hard ones we have encountered in our journey. The truth that we will never fully be at one with ourselves and that our necessarily imperfect self-knowledge will always constrict and distort our knowledge of the world. The truth that no "alternative" path to esoteric wisdom exists to release us from the intrinsic uncertainties of human knowledge and action. The truth that the beauty of the innocent must be protected by the less deceived, who must also disarm them, and that idle fantasies of stopping or reversing time's wheel only block the path to a decent future. And then perhaps the hardest truth: that no stratagem for keeping knowledge at bay can ever relieve us of responsibility for our actions. Who would not be tempted to take flight in the face of such an onslaught? Anyone who does not feel sympathy for *homo fugiens* truly is an innocent.

Let us then in parting consider the young man in the cave one last time and imagine his situation differently, in a way that brings it closer to our own. Let us imagine that, after leading the boy and man out of the darkness, the female stranger did not deposit them in a clearing where they could spend their days contemplating the Ideas. Instead she led them to a pebbly shore with little rowboats dotting it, there for the taking.

Looking out over the water, they could just make out the coasts of different islands. The weather was heavy, which meant the rowing would not be easy and they might not even make it. And who knows what they would find on those islands—friend or foe, lakes or deserts, food or famine—or whether they could ever return. The man is eager to set out and jumps in. But the boy hesitates. Should he venture out without knowing where he might end up? Is it worth the risk? Or should he return to the familiar cave where he felt protected? What should he do?

What would you do? Think very hard before answering that question.

Notes

INTRODUCTION

3 *"The faintest of all human passions"*: Introduction to
   Manlius, *Astronomicon*, vol. 1 (Cambridge, UK, 1903),
   xliii.

5 *"all human beings want to know"*: Aristotle, *Metaphys-*
   ics, in J. Barnes, ed., *Collected Works of Aristotle*, vol. 1
   (Princeton, NJ, 1984), 980a.

6 *"Ignorance is bliss"*: The source of that proverb is the
   poem by the eighteenth-century English writer Thomas
   Gray, "Ode on a Distant Prospect at Eton College." It
   speaks in the voice of a grown man who returns to his
   old boarding school and falls into a reverie about the
   young students playing in the fields, unaware of what life
   holds in store for them.

> The thoughtless day, the easy night,
> The spirits pure, the slumbers light, . . .
> Regardless of their doom
> The little victims play!

For now, the narrator thinks, these children are protected from what he calls *the vultures of the mind*: envy,
despair, ambition, remorse, and above all awareness of
old age and death. And so, he asks, why should we ever
disabuse them?

> Yet ah! why should they know their fate?
> Since sorrow never comes too late,
>   And happiness too swiftly flies.

> Thought would destroy their paradise.
> No more; where ignorance is bliss,
>   'Tis folly to be wise.

6 *a small LED screen*: Moshe Halbertal, *Concealment and Revelation: Esotericism in Jewish Thought and Its Philosophical Implications*, trans. J. Feldman (Princeton, 2007), chapter 17.

9 *"an apparently opposite drive"*: Friedrich Nietzsche, *Beyond Good and Evil*, trans. W. Kaufman (New York, 1966), §230.

10 *"The self wants to be great"*: Blaise Pascal, *Pensées* (Sellier, ed.), trans. R. Ariew (Indianapolis, 2005), §743.

ON EVASION

21 *"O Oedipus"*: Sophocles, *Oedipus the King*, trans. D. Grene (Chicago, 1942), 1065–70.

23 *"You are the land's pollution"*: Sophocles, *Oedipus the King*, 350–55.

23 *"I beg you"*: Sophocles, *Oedipus the King*, 1060–65.

EVASIVE ACTION

25 *"There is no self-knowledge"*: Thomas Mann, "Culture and Socialism" (1927), in Thomas Mann, *Past Masters*, trans. H. T. Lowe-Porter (New York, 1933), 204.

25 *Among the recent discoveries of neuroscience*: See generally William Hirstein, *Brain Fiction: Self-Deception and the Riddle of Confabulation* (Cambridge, MA, 2004). The description of syndromes is found on p. 12.

27 *Recall the biblical story*: 2 Samuel 11–12.

30 *"Everything on which I set my gaze"*: Augustine, *Confessions*, trans. H. Chadwick (Oxford, UK, 1991), 4.9–12.

30 *"The mind commands"*: Augustine, *Confessions*, 8.21.

31 *"There was a grand struggle"*: Augustine, *Confessions*, 8.19, 8.22.

31 *"Grant me chastity"*: Augustine, *Confessions*, 8.17.

31 *"While he was speaking"*: Augustine, *Confessions*, 8.16.

JAILBREAK

33 *"In the fight"*: Franz Kafka, *Zürau Aphorisms* (New York, 2006), §52. My translation.

33 *"If any man be in Christ"*: 2 Corinthians 5:17.

38 *"Today neurosis"*: Sigmund Freud, *Five Lectures on Psycho-Analysis*, trans. J. Strachey (New York, 1961), 56.

39 *"has as much influence"*: Sigmund Freud, "'Wild' Psycho-Analysis," in *The Standard Edition of the Complete Psychological Works of Sigmund Freud*, vol. 11 (London, 1952–1974), 225.

ZIPPERS

44 *Consider Cephalus*: Plato, *Republic*, trans. A. Bloom (New York, 1968), 327a–331d.

50 *After that, Socrates told the jury*: Plato, *Apology*, in *The Dialogues of Plato*, trans. R. E. Allen, vol. 1 (New Haven, 1984), 21d–e.

BARSTOOLS

52 *"Disillusion as the last illusion"*: Wallace Stevens, "An Ordinary Evening in New Haven," in F. Kermode and J. Richardson, eds., *Wallace Stevens: Collected Poetry and Prose* (New York, 1997), 399.

53 *"Hatred of argument"*: Plato, *Phaedo*, trans. E. Brann et al. (Newburyport, MA, 1998), 89d–90c.

54 *"Mind is the cause of all things"*: Plato, *Phaedo*, 97c.

55 *A Greek rhetorician named Thrasymachus*: Plato, *Republic*, 336b–354a.

ON TABOO

61 *"Too much truth"*: Pascal, *Pensées*, §230.

61 *"The roof that keeps out the rain"*: André Gide, *Paludes*, Folio edition (Paris, 1920), 136–37.

61 *"What do I have when I don't have it all?"*: Friedrich Schiller, "Das verschleierte Bild zu Sais" (1795). I have

slightly revised the translation of Ernst Gombrich in P. Horden, ed., *The Symbol of the Veil* (London, 1985), 75–109.

THE CABINET OF DR. SALAZAR

73 *"an acute attack of integrity"*: The quotations in this paragraph are drawn from Henrik Ibsen, *The Wild Duck*, Dover edition (Mineola, NY, 2000), 53–76.

THE WHIRLWIND

77 *"Only Zeus is free"*: Aeschylus, *Prometheus Bound*, trans. D. Grene (Chicago, 1956), 50.

80 *"You have found favor"*: Exodus 33:17.

80 *"You shall see my back"*: Exodus 33:23.

81 *"What has Jehovah your God asked of you"*: Deuteronomy 10:12. Subsequent quotations: Psalm 2:11, Psalm 147:11, Jeremiah 31:3, Psalm 86:15.

83 *"Where were you"*: Job 38:4.

83 *"I have uttered"*: Job 42:3.

86 *"Wisdom cries aloud in the street"*: Proverbs 1:20–22.

THE DEVIL'S BRIDE

89 *"There is then in philosophy"*: Clement of Alexandria, *Stromata*, in A. Roberts et al., eds., *Ante-Nicene Fathers*, vol. 2 (Buffalo, NY, 1885), 1.5–1.17.

89 *"But the devil's bride"*: Martin Luther, "Last Wittenberg Sermon" (1546), in J. Pelikan et al., eds., *Luther's Works*, vol. 52 (Minneapolis, 1957), 374.

90 *"the most eminent saint"*: Karl Marx, "The Difference Between the Democritean and Epicurean Philosophy of Nature" (1841), in *Marx-Engels Collected Works*, vol. 1 (Moscow, 1902), final line of Foreword.

90 *"man's greatest friend"*: Friedrich Nietzsche, *The Birth of Tragedy*, trans. R. Spiers (Cambridge, UK, 1999), §3.

92 *"Depravity exults"*: Pope Gregory XVI, *Mirari Vos: On Liberalism and Religious Indifferentism* (1832), §5. Downloadable at papalencyclicals.net.

95 *"Hope is a good breakfast"*: Francis Bacon, "Apoph-thegms contained in *Resuscitatio*," in *The Works of Francis Bacon*, vol. 7 (London, 1859), §36.

100 *A survey of American doctors*: Donald Oken, "What to Tell Cancer Patients: A Study of Medical Attitudes," *Journal of the American Medical Association* 175 (1961): 1120–28.

ON EMPTINESS

105 *"Truth, Sir, is a cow"*: James Boswell, *Boswell's Life of Samuel Johnson*, ed. G. B. Hill, vol. 1 (New York, 1889), 514.

106 *"It is of great use to the sailor"*: John Locke, *An Essay Concerning Human Understanding* (London, 1689), 1.1.8.

107 *"Now we have eaten of the tree of knowledge"*: Heinrich von Kleist, *Selected Writings*, ed. D. Constantine (London, 1997), 413.

THE BAGPIPE AND THE SAGE

110 *"It is a foolish custom"*: Thomas Hobbes, *English Works*, ed. Molesworth (London, 1840), 4:448.

111 *"wait upon the Lord"*: Isaiah 40:31.

115 *Mormon missionaries are apparently taught*: See, for example, Hugh Nibley, *The Prophetic Book of Mormon* (Salt Lake City, UT, 1989), 221–22.

118 *the more authentic voice of God*: On this psychological paradox, see Moses Maimonides, *The Guide of the Perplexed*, trans. S. Pines, vol. 2 (Chicago, 1963), 3.31, 523–24.

118 *"You will not recognize the writing"*: Irene Richardson, *Learn How to Do Automatic Writing: A Step by Step Course to Help You Access Higher Realms of the Mind, Body and Spirit* (Frederick, MD, 2008), 8–9.

THIS LITTLE LIGHT OF MINE

119 *"Where now is Greece"*: John Chrysostom, "On the Acts of the Apostles," in P. Schaff, ed., *Nicene and Post-*

Nicene Fathers, First Series, vol. 11 (Buffalo, NY, 1889), Homily 4.

120 *"For Christ sent me not to baptize"*: 1 Corinthians 1:17–25.

122 *The* iurodivye, *as they were called*: The names can be found in Sergey A. Ivanov, *Holy Fools in Byzantium and Beyond* (Oxford, UK, 2006), which is also an excellent survey of this subject.

125 *"restrain the inopportune raving"*: John Chrysostom, "On the Incomprehensibility of God," quoted in Ivanov, *Holy Fools in Byzantium and Beyond*, 22.

126 *"Yet among the mature"*: 1 Corinthians 2:6–15.

LEGION

130 *"In the back of the large auditorium"*: Frank Hammond and Ida Mae Hammond, *Pigs in the Parlor: A Practical Guide to Deliverance* (Kirkwood, MO, 1973), 43–44.

130 *"go in and out of our bodies"*: Robert Burton, *The Anatomy of Melancholy,* ed. H. Jackson (London, 1932), 200.

131 *"What have you to do with me, Jesus"*: Mark 5:1–13, Luke 8:27–33.

133 *To meet a new demand for exorcisms*: See generally Brian Levack, *The Devil Within: Possession & Exorcism in the Christian West* (New Haven, 2013). On Italy, see Lorenzo Cresci, "In Italia boom di richieste per liberarsi dal diavolo, ma mancano gli esorcisti," *La Stampa* (September 25, 2016). On Indianapolis, see Mike Mariani, "American Exorcism," *The Atlantic* (December 2018).

133 *"even Satan disguises himself"*: 2 Corinthians 11:14.

134 *"It is one of God's"*: Aldous Huxley, *The Devils of Loudun* (New York, 1952), 240. For a vivid account of the seventeenth-century Jesuit exorcist Surin and his role in the famous alleged demon possessions among nuns in Loudun, France, see Michel de Certeau, *The Possession at Loudun* (Chicago, 2000).

BRUISED FRUIT

138 *"A poet is someone"*: Randall Jarrell, "Reflections on Wallace Stevens," in *No Other Book: Selected Essays* (New York, 1999), 122.

139 *"I write when commanded"*: Recorded in Henry Crabb Robinson, *Diary, Reminiscences, and Correspondence*, vol. 2 (Boston, 1869), 35.

139 *"The god takes the mind"*: Plato, *Ion*, in *The Dialogues of Plato*, trans. R. E. Allen, vol. 3 (New Haven, CT, 1996), 534d.

141 *a fictional letter he published*: Hugo von Hofmannsthal, *The Lord Chandos Letters and Other Writings*, trans. J. Rotenberg (New York, 2005), 117–38.

ON INNOCENCE

145 *"Innocence is like a dumb leper"*: Graham Greene, *The Quiet American* (London, 1955), 40.

145 *Before setting out for Moriah*: Genesis 22:1–19.

146 *"Behold the Lamb of God"*: John 1:29.

146 *"brought as a lamb to the slaughter"*: Isaiah 53:7.

146 *"good shepherd"*: John 11:1–18.

148 *"Hide us from the face"*: Revelation 6:16.

149 *"the city has no need of sun"*: Revelation 21:23.

149 *"The modest Rose"*: William Blake, "The Lilly" from *Songs of Innocence and Experience*, in D. V. Erdman, ed., *The Complete Poetry and Prose of William Blake*, newly revised edition (New York, 1988), 25.

PEARS

150 *"Eternal wisdom goes"*: Angelus Silesius, *The Cherubinic Wanderer* (1657), trans. M. Shrady (New York, 1986), 1.165.

152 *the Child . . . is the best copy of Adam*: John Earle, *Microcosmographie* (1628), quoted in George Boas, *The Cult of Childhood* (London, 1966), 42–43.

152 *"What children we still are, Kolya!"*: Fyodor Dosto-
evsky, *The Idiot*, trans. R. Pevear and L. Volokhonsky
(New York, 2003), 512.

153 *"Come to me"*: Quoted in Sarah Iles Johnston, "Charming Children: The Use of the Child in Ancient Divination," *Arethusa* 34, no. 1 (Winter 2001): 102.

153 *A similar scene is recounted*: Luke 2:41–52.

155 *"A seven-year-old child"*: Michel Houellebecq, *Submis-
sion* (New York, 2015), 228.

156 *In the Second Book of Kings*: 2 Kings 2:23–24.

156 *Infancy Gospel of Thomas*: In J. K. Elliott, ed., *The
Apocryphal New Testament* (Oxford, UK, 1993),
68–83.

157 *"So tiny a child"*: Augustine, *Confessions*, 1.19.

157 *"I had no motive"*: Augustine, *Confessions*, 2.9.

158 *"After an account"*: Ellen Key, *The Century of the Child*
(New York, 1909), 112.

PUTTI

159 *"Prudery is the pretension"*: Friedrich Schlegel, *Athe-
naeum Fragments* (1798), in *Philosophical Fragments*,
trans. P. Firchow (Minneapolis, 1991), §31.

160 *One of the earliest*: *Comédies de Térence rendues très-
hônnetes en y changeant fort peu de choses*, trans. P. R.
Tibour (1687).

160 *Masturbation is a good example*: I have drawn from
Henry Jenkins, "The Sensuous Child," in H. Jenkins, ed.,
Children's Culture Reader (New York, 1998), 209–30;
Beth Bailey, "The Vexed History of Children and Sex," in
P. S. Fass, ed., *The Routledge History of Childhood in
the Western World* (London, 2012), 191–210; and Mar-
jorie Heins, *Not in Front of the Children: "Indecency,"
Censorship, and the Innocence of Youth* (New Bruns-
wick, NJ, 2007).

163 *"Do I put makeup on her?"*: Laura Goode, "I Was a
Teenage Pageant Star," *New York Magazine* (November
14, 2012).

164 *"O sweet and sacred Childhood"*: Guerric of Igny (twelfth-century monk), quoted in John Saward, *Perfect Fools: Folly for Christ's Sake in Catholic and Orthodox Spirituality* (Oxford, UK, 2000), 64.

WOLVES

167 *"For paradise to be possible"*: Hans Blumenberg, *Löwen* (Berlin, 2010). My translation. See also Hans Blumenberg, *Lions*, trans. K. Driscoll (London, 2017), 54.

169 *Consider the case*: Elissa Wall, *Stolen Innocence: My Story of Growing Up in a Polygamous Sect, Becoming a Teenage Bride, and Breaking Free of Warren Jeffs* (New York, 2008). The documentary *Prophets Prey* (2015) paints a chilling portrait of the Fundamentalist Church of Jesus Christ of Latter-Day Saints in which Wall was raised.

171 *"If any one comes to me"*: Luke 14:26.

172 *"Love your enemies"*: Matthew 5:44, 5:39, 6:34.

174 *"Where is the moral Switzerland?"*: Uwe Johnson, *Anniversaries*, trans. D. Searls (New York, 2018), 332.

175 *"darkness was upon"*: Genesis 1:2.

176 *"Their singleness"*: Elizabeth Bowen, *The Death of the Heart* (London, 1939), 144–45.

THE VERY RICH HOURS OF SAMUEL PICKWICK, ESQ.

178 *"To be no longer innocent"*: W. H. Auden, *The Dyer's Hand* (London, 1948), 409.

184 *"Perhaps everybody has a Garden of Eden"*: James Baldwin, *Giovanni's Room* (New York, 2000), 25.

ON NOSTALGIA

187 *"You will never be again"*: Theodor Storm, "Vor Tag," in *Gedichte*, ed. G. Grimm (Ditzingen, Germany, 2021). My translation.

187 *"Nothing is more sweet"*: Homer, *Odyssey*, trans. R. Lattimore (New York, 1967), 9.33.

188 *"The land of your ancestors"*: Virgil, *The Aeneid*, trans. A. Mandelbaum (New York, 1971), 3.125–214.

THE FAMILY ALBUM

190 *"When you go looking"*: Eudora Welty, "The Wide Net," in *Selected Stories of Eudora Welty* (New York, 1943), 54.

190 *In the early seventeenth century*: Jean Starobinski and William S. Kemp, "The Idea of Nostalgia," *Diogenes* 14, no. 54 (1966): 81–103.

194 *It is always surprising to learn*: Hugh Trevor-Roper, "The Invention of Tradition: The Highland Tradition of Scotland," in E. Hobsbawm and T. Ranger, eds., *The Invention of Tradition* (Cambridge, UK, 1983), 15–41.

194 *"Yes, sir"*: Boswell, *Boswell's Life of Samuel Johnson*, 458.

195 *"kosher Jewish tartan"*: Stephen Erlanger, "Kosher Kilts and Plaid Skullcaps: Scotland's Jews Get a Tartan," *New York Times* (March 31, 2016).

ABOUT FACE

196 *"The rule is, jam tomorrow"*: Lewis Carroll, *Through the Looking-Glass and What Alice Found There* (London, 1872), 94.

199 *"Who knows"*: Georg Christoph Lichtenberg, *The Waste Books*, trans. R. J. Hollingdale (New York, 2000), Notebook K (1793–1796), §82.

201 *Cato the Elder*: See Plutarch, "Marcus Cato," in *Lives of the Noble Greeks and Romans*, trans. B. Perrin (Cambridge, UK, 1914), §§22–23.

204 *"In the West"*: Ivan Kireevsky, "On the Nature of European Culture and on Its Relationship to Russian Culture" (1852), in B. Jakim and R. Bird, eds., *On Spiritual Unity: A Slavophile Reader* (Hudson, NY, 1998), 187–232.

204 *"the obvious incongruity"*: Muhamad Asad (Leopold Weiss), *Islam at the Crossroads* (Delhi, 1937), 3. For this section I have drawn entirely on this and other works of Islamist historiography, especially Abdul Hassan Ali Nadwi, *Islam and the World: The Rise and Decline of the Muslims and Its Effect on Mankind* (Leicester, UK, 1978), and Sayyid Qutb, *Milestones* (Delhi, 2006).

208 *"In her Raqqa diary"*: Robyn Creswell and Bernard Haykel, "Battle Lines," *The New Yorker* (June 8, 2015).

CIVIS ROMANUS SUM

209 *"For who can doubt"*: Petrarch, "Letter to Giovanni Colonna," in *Francesco Petrarca, Rerum familiarum Libri I-VIII*, trans. A. S. Bernardo (Albany, NY, 1975), 6.2.

209 *"It would have been easier"*: Ernst Bloch, *On Karl Marx* (New York, 1971), 33.

211 *"The Rome that we contemplate"*: Benito Mussolini, speech delivered April 21, 1922, in *Opera omnia*, vol. 18 (Florence, 1956), 160. My translation.

213 *"I accept the view"*: Tacitus, *Germania*, in *Agricola and Germania*, trans. H. Manningly (London, 2009), §4.

213 *"a bible that every thinking German"*: Quoted in Christopher B. Krebs, *A Most Dangerous Book: Tacitus's Germania from the Roman Empire to the Third Reich* (New York, 2012), 217.

216 *"Greeks and Romans become so close"*: Adolf Hitler, speech on September 1, 1933, quoted in Johann Chapoutot, *Greeks, Romans, Germans: How the Nazis Usurped Europe's Classical Past* (Berkeley, CA, 2016), 153.

216 *Alfred Bäumler*: Chapoutot, *Greeks, Romans, Germans*, 113.

THE WRINKLED CHILD

217 *"The god of Regret"*: Antonio Tabucchi, *Woman of Porto Pim*, trans. T. Parks (Brooklyn, NY, 2013), 5.

219 *"When a belief vanishes"*: Marcel Proust, *Swann's Way*, trans. C. K. Scott Moncrieff and T. Kilmartin, revised by D. J. Enright (New York, 1998), 603.

ENVOI

223 *"Light, light, more light!"*: Miguel de Unamuno, *The Tragic Sense of Life*, trans. J. E. Crawford Flitch (London, 1921), 327.

Acknowledgments

I am grateful for past support from the Institut d'études avancées (Paris), the Institut für die Wissenschaften vom Menschen (Vienna), and the Russell Sage Foundation (New York City). Special thanks for much needed encouragement—and, occasionally, discouragement—over the years to Sarah Chalfant, Eric Chinski, Alex Star, Damon Linker, Andrew Stark, Lejb Fogelman, Leon Wieseltier, James Lasdun, George Packer, Hans Sluga, Darrin McMahon, and Edna Ullman-Margalit (1946–2010), who planted the seed.

A NOTE ABOUT THE AUTHOR

Mark Lilla is Professor of Humanities at Columbia
University and a contributor to *The New York Review
of Books*, *Liberties*, and other publications worldwide.
His books include *The Once and Future Liberal: After
Identity Politics*; *The Shipwrecked Mind: On Political
Reaction*; *The Stillborn God: Religion, Politics, and
the Modern West*; and *The Reckless Mind: Intellectu-
als in Politics*. He lives in New York City.